Dedication

To my daughters Shakuntala and Savitri, my grandsons Arjuna and Rama
— and anyone who wants to turn out compact tasty meals but not always in a hurry.

Contents

Introduction

A one-dish meal is by definition a meal comprising just one dish that contains protein, vegetables and carbohydrates so that the dish makes a complete meal. There are any number of reasons to do one-dish meals not least because many are easy to put together, to carry around, and make perfect contributions to pot-luck meals. Ease of preparation be it for a simple family meal or a dinner with friends is always desirable. All cooks love quick and tasty meals but also appreciate the ability to prepare everything or most things ahead of time. It simplifies the task of hosting and leaves you free to enjoy your guests or get on with other tasks. A one-dish meal may have everything cooked together and served as one or it may consist of different cooked or raw ingredients combined into one in the kitchen or at the table either by the host or guests themselves. Asian one-dish meals are particularly flexible because many consist of several items that have to be combined to make the dish. With some particularly festive dishes, putting it all together is also left to the guests. And many Asian one dish-meals are perfect ways to use up leftovers be it rice, meat or seafood or small quantities of vegetables. Some even call for pre-cooked meat and seafood, again allowing for advance preparation.

While the list of ingredients can look daunting, one way to ease the preparation of even the most complicated one-dish meal is to have ready various cooked ingredients that keep well or which can be kept frozen. Ready-to-use stock makes quick noodle soups and rice soups. Another way to simplify preparation is to always prepare double or even treble quantities of ingredients like stock, spice mixes or garnishes. Stock and spice pastes freeze very well and garnishes like fried garlic and shallots, roasted nuts and toasted sesame seeds store well in the refrigerator. Even basic dressings can be mixed ahead in a large enough quantity and kept against the day when you must have a tasty salad but are not up to pounding and messing about with more than a few ingredients.

A cookbook has to specify ingredients and quantities. What kind of a cookbook would it be if it did not? However, don't be put off by what looks like precise measurements. The wonderful thing about many Asian one-dish meals is that you can wing it to suit personal preferences. If you prefer less carbohydrates, reduce the quantity of rice or noodles. If you want more vegetables or have more guests, increase the seasoning and quantities. A little more or less of something will not be a disaster. And if you have a small tomato rather than one that weighs 100 g (3$\frac{1}{2}$ oz), just use what you do have. Or if the capsicum is very big, it won't matter much if you use it all up. The other thing to remember is that you can make it easier by substituting certain categories of ingredients for something you already have in the fridge or freezer. For instance, chicken and pork are interchangeable. No dark soy sauce? Use light soy sauce but remember that the colour is much lighter and light soy sauce is more salty than dark soy sauce. No light soy sauce? Use fish sauce but remember that the dish will end up with a distinct fish tang that you won't get with light soy sauce. Japanese and Chinese soy sauces do not taste alike but one can be substituted for the other in practically most dishes. Many vegetables can be substituted to suit personal taste, reduced or even left out. Not everyone likes lots of garlic or onions. Reduce or substitute for something milder like spring onions. The end-result will still be tasty.

Naturally, there will be a trade-off with some substitutes. If you use chicken instead of pork bones to make Penang Hokkien *mee* soup, it will not have the authentic hawker food flavour. Substituting light soy sauce for fish sauce in *yam woon sen* (Thai glass noodle salad) will give you a glass noodle salad but not *yam woon sen*. Fish sauce is an essential part of Thai food. However, not everything can be substituted particularly the different roots and spices that go into the spice paste and make the dish Thai, Straits Chinese, Burmese or whatever.

Speed and ease of preparation are not the only considerations in preparing an Asian one-dish meal. A one-dish party meal has built-in flexibility. It can be quickly expanded to handle unexpected numbers. Guests can put together their own combinations to suit their personal taste. Some dishes can even handle vegetarians and carnivores simultaneously. Dining times are flexible, too, if the party is one where guests flow in and out. A one-dish meal such as Gado-Gado is perfect for guests who show up at different times as it even tastes fine cold. If the dish is one that should be served hot, the gravy or soup is easily heated up again. Reheating many of the dishes do not have adverse effects on the flavours. Different permutations are possible with many one-dish party meals. Quite a number of noodle dishes fit into this flexible category as do certain types of wraps that are combined with plain boiled rice or boiled rice noodles.

While the ingredients are specified in the recipes to achieve a certain flavour, there are notes for substitutions and shortcuts. In fact, the front section titled The Basics has recipes for many shortcuts. It gives recipes for some basic ingredients, garnishes and even side dishes that can be prepared days or weeks ahead and refrigerated or frozen. Ingredients such as stock and spice pastes can be made at your convenience or if you have some leftover roots, chillies and suchlike sitting around and drying out. The section after The Basics focuses on family meals although a number of dishes also make good one-dish party meals. The last section focuses on one-dish party meals which will take more effort and time to put together, but will give your guests something to do and talk about.

The Basics

Many of these basic condiments are available in supermarkets,
wet markets and Asian stores everywhere, but most are easy to make at home
and cost less, while some such as *sambal belacan* should be made
at home so you can control the taste and flavour.

Toasted Nuts

Peanuts, almonds, cashew nuts and pine nuts are the most useful nuts for Asian dishes. Skinned peanuts are worth the little extra as skinning toasted peanuts is a messy business. Nuts can be toasted by dry-frying in a pan, grilled under a low grill or baked in a slow oven (120°C / 250°F). Roasting in a combination microwave oven with a baking function halves the time for slow-cooking almonds, cashews and peanuts. Pine nuts are best dry-fried in a pan over low heat to a pale gold. It takes only a few minutes. Be careful not to over-brown or nuts will be bitter. Turn off the heat as soon as the colour begins to change. The residual heat will turn them golden. Except for dry-frying in a wok which requires constant stirring, nuts being grilled, microwaved or baked need to be turned over every 10 minutes or so at the start and more frequently when they colour. Do the taste test to check when nuts are done. Chopping or pounding nuts just before use will release better flavour. Cool, bag and store roasted nuts in the fridge or freezer.

Toasted Grated Coconut

Makes about 250 g (9 oz)

Make this with canned desiccated coconut or with freshly grated coconut. If using canned desiccated coconut, the frying time will be considerably reduced, but the amount will remain about the same. However, if using fresh grated coconut, the amount of toasted coconut will be reduced to a little over half that of the wet coconut. It keeps well in the fridge or freezer. Toasted coconut is a good substitute for ground toasted peanuts in many Asian salads.

Fresh grated skinned coconut	500 g (1 lb 1$\frac{1}{2}$ oz) or 250 g (9 oz) desiccated coconut

1. In a dry wok, dry-fry grated coconut, whether fresh or desiccated over low heat, stir-frying continuously. It burns very easily, so do not leave it unattended at any time.
2. Store refrigerated or frozen as it is or finely ground before storing.

Tamarind Juice

Makes about 250 ml (8 fl oz / 1 cup)

Mix 140 g (5 oz) tamarind paste with 250 ml (8 fl oz) water in a glass bottle and refrigerate. The juice keeps for months. Strain out what is needed. Top up with paste and water as necessary.

Chopped Raw Garlic in Oil

Keep this basic ingredient handy in a glass bottle in the fridge together with a small spoon and you are ready to stir-fry many things at the drop of a hat. Chop a head or even two of peeled garlic in a food processor, bottle and cover the garlic with cooking oil. The oil stops the garlic odour from permeating the fridge. Bottled this way, chopped raw garlic keeps for weeks.

Fried Garlic and Garlic Oil

Makes 1 cup

Like shallot oil and fried shallots, garlic oil and fried garlic are used to give instant flavour to many dishes. The fried garlic and the oil can be bottled together if preferred although there may be times when more of one is preferred. Note that garlic browns much more quickly than shallots and low heat is preferred to high heat.

Garlic	150 g (5 oz), peeled
Cooking oil	250 ml (8 fl oz / 1 cup)

1. Chop garlic in a food processor until fairly fine but not mushy. If food processor does not chop without any liquid or turns it into mush, hand-chop garlic.
2. Heat oil in a wok and add chopped garlic. Stir continuously until garlic begins to turn a nice shade of yellow. Turn down heat if garlic is browning unevenly.
3. About 1 minute before colour is ideal, turn off heat but continue stirring until garlic is golden brown.
4. To simplify things, bottle both garlic and oil together. Refrigerate to extend shelf life.

Fried Shallots and Shallot Oil

Makes 1 cup

Frying sliced shallots in oil gives you both shallot oil and fried shallots. Both the oil and the fried shallots give instant flavour to numerous one-dish meals as well as make a great dressing for blanched vegetables. Ready-to-use fried shallots are sold in Singapore wet markets and supermarkets. It is also carried in some Asian stores abroad.

Cooking oil	250 ml (8 fl oz / 1 cup)
Shallots	150 g (5$\frac{1}{3}$ oz), peeled and thinly sliced

1. Heat oil in a wok and add shallots when oil is hot. Keeping heat at medium, stir-fry continuously until shallots are crisp and golden.
2. Turn down heat if shallots start to brown too quickly while still wet and soft. To get a nice golden brown, watch the heat and colour carefully. When shallots are a pale yellow, turn heat off but continue stirring until colour deepens. Turn heat off and stir until shallots stop changing colour.
3. The bulk of the shallots can be stored apart from the oil. Scoop shallots out.
4. Bottle cooled oil and store in the fridge to extend shelf life.

Spice Mixes

If the ground spices are very fresh, the spice mix will keep for at least a year or more in the fridge. To make your own ground spices to ensure freshness, dry the spice in a frying pan over low heat or toast in a slow oven until crisp but not burnt. Pound and sift using a fine wire sieve. Repeat the pounding and sifting until the spice is all fine. While coriander, cumin and fennel are easy to pound to powder, some spices like cinnamon and cloves are very difficult without special equipment. Ginger poses a different problem. It is easy to pound but not easy to dry to a powder without special equipment. Buy such spices already ground. To make the spice mixes, mix the ground spices together and bottle. Label and refrigerate for a longer shelf life.

Baharat (Iraqi Spice Mix)

Makes about ¹/₂ cup

Ground paprika	3 Tbsp	Ground ginger	1 tsp
Ground black pepper	2 Tbsp	Ground cloves	¹/₂ tsp
Ground cumin	1 tsp	Ground cardamom	¹/₂ tsp
Ground coriander	1 tsp	Ground nutmeg	¹/₄ tsp
Ground turmeric	1 tsp		

Advieh (Persian Spice Mix)

Makes about ¹/₂ cup

Ground cinnamon	¹/₂ Tbsp	Ground green cardamom	3 tsp
Ground nutmeg	¹/₂ Tbsp	Ground cumin	3 tsp
Ground rose petals	1 Tbsp	Ground pistachios	3 Tbsp

Indian Garam Masala

Makes about ¹/₂ cup

Ground coriander	1 Tbsp	Ground cardamom	3 tsp
Ground fennel	1 Tbsp	Ground cinnamon	3 tsp
Ground ginger	1 Tbsp	Ground cloves	2 tsp
Ground cumin	¹/₂ Tbsp		

Sambal Belacan

Makes about ³/₄ cup

This Malay/Straits Chinese condiment is to be distinguished from *belacan* or prawn paste. *Sambal belacan* is a combination of fresh red chillies pounded with toasted dried prawn paste. *Sambal belacan* tastes best pounded in a mortar and pestle rather than blended in a food processor. However, the chillies can be coarsely chopped in a food chopper to reduce pounding time. *Sambal belacan* keeps well in the fridge for up to a month. It can also be frozen in serving sizes. Use firm Penang-style prawn paste that comes in a block that is firm enough to cut rather than the liquid variety in a jar.

Red chillies	150 g (5¹/₃ oz), seeded
Dried prawn paste (*belacan*)	45 g (1¹/₂ oz / 3 Tbsp)

1. Chop chillies coarsely in a food processor.
2. If toasting prawn paste on a grill or in an oven-toaster, press it into a thin flat piece first. Toast both sides until slightly brown. Be careful not to burn it or the *sambal* will taste bitter. The prawn paste can also be "toasted" by dry-frying crumbled pieces in a wok until slightly brown. Stir constantly when dry-frying.
3. Pound chopped chillies and toasted prawn paste in a mortar and pestle to a paste.
4. Store in a glass bottle in the fridge or frozen in small portions. Defrost only what is needed.

Sambal Belacan with Lime Juice

Makes about ¹/₃ cup

Sambal belacan with lime juice keeps well in the fridge but a fresh condiment can also be made with frozen *sambal belacan*.

Sambal belacan (page 13)	2 Tbsp
Lime juice	3 Tbsp

1. Mix together. Bottle and store in the fridge.

Cooked Dried Red Chilli Paste

This chilli paste is basic to quite a number of Asian dishes and makes a good condiment as well. The hardest part is seeding the dried chillies. Cooked dried chilli paste freezes well and is easy to cut off chunks if the jar is partially defrosted. The paste takes well to being defrosted and refrozen. Alternatively, bottle the cooked chilli paste, cover it with oil and store refrigerated. The oil acts as a preservative and can be used in the cooking or as chilli oil to perk up a bland dish in place of chilli flakes.

Dried red chillies	500 g (1 lb 1¹/₂ oz), seeded
Water	125 ml (4 fl oz / ¹/₂ cup)
Cooking oil	125 ml (4 fl oz / ¹/₂ cup)
Salt	1 tsp

1. Rinse seeded chillies well, then soak in clean water until soft. Blend softened chillies with 125 ml (4 fl oz / ¹/₂ cup) water to a fine paste.
2. Spoon chilli paste into a large oven-proof dish with a cover. It should not be more than three-quarters full, preferably less.
3. Stir in oil and salt.
4. Cover dish and microwave chilli paste for about 20 minutes, taking care to stir paste every 5 minutes. If paste is too dry, stir in some water.
5. Cool paste, then box it and store in the freezer until needed.

Cooked Oil Dressing

Makes 125 ml (4 fl oz / ¹/₂ cup)

The flavour of this dressing will depend on what was cooked in the oil. Even oil used to fry fish can be used if you want a fishy flavour.

Dried prawn paste (*belacan*)	¹/₂ tsp
Tamarind paste	25 g (1 oz)
Water	4 Tbsp
Cooked oil	4 Tbsp
Fish sauce	3 Tbsp
White sesame seeds	1 Tbsp, toasted and pounded

1. Dry-fry prawn paste and when well-toasted, press with a spoon to a powder. Mix tamarind paste and water together. Strain off and discard solids. Place in a glass jar with prawn paste powder and the other ingredients and shake. Refrigerate until needed.

Indo-Chinese Dressing

Makes about 125 ml (4 fl oz / ½ cup)

This dressing keeps well in the refrigerator because of the salty fish sauce.

Garlic	3 cloves, peeled
Red bird's eye chillies	8, seeded
Fish sauce	4 Tbsp
Large lime juice	4 Tbsp
Sugar	1 Tbsp

1. Pound garlic and chillies to a paste, then mix with fish sauce, lime juice and sugar. Adjust seasoning to taste when using the dressing.

Red Chilli-vinegar Sauce

Makes about 250 ml (8 fl oz / 1 cup)

Red chillies	150 g (5⅓ oz), seeded
Ginger	3 slices
Salt	1 tsp
Sugar	1 Tbsp
Chinese white rice vinegar	4 Tbsp

1. Grind all ingredients together in a food processor until fine.
2. Bottle and rest sauce for several hours before consuming. This sauce keeps well when refrigerated.

Red Chillies with Soy Sauce / Fish Sauce

This is a standard condiment for noodle soups, rice soups, fried rice and noodles. Substitute light soy sauce with fish sauce if serving a Thai-style dish.

Red chillies	to taste, seeded and thinly sliced
Light soy sauce/fish sauce	to taste

1. Put desired amount of chillies in a small dip saucer.
2. Add light soy sauce/fish sauce to taste.

Vinegar-chilli Dip

Makes about ¼ cup

To make this an Indo-Chinese-style dip, substitute light soy sauce with fish sauce.

Fish sauce/light soy sauce	2 Tbsp
White rice vinegar	2 Tbsp
Bird's eye chillies	6, chopped

1. Combine ingredients in a small dip saucer.

Shichimi Togarashi (Seven-flavour Chilli)

Makes about ¼ cup

A common condiment sprinkled on Japanese noodles is a mix of seven ingredients known as *shichimi togarashi* or seven-flavour chilli, ground chillies being the dominant ingredient. Often just called *shichimi*, this condiment is available from Japanese supermarkets. There are different combinations of seven or more ingredients and in Japan there are shops that will make up the condiment to suit the customer's taste. Put together your own, especially if you already have some bottled ground seaweed condiment handy. Instead of mandarin orange peel, you can also use orange or lemon peel. *Shichimi* is also good with Korean food.

White sesame seeds	$1^1/_2$ Tbsp
Black sesame seeds	1 Tbsp
Mandarin orange peel	$^1/_2$ tsp, finely chopped
Ground seaweed	1 tsp
Mustard powder	$^1/_2$ tsp
Ground ginger	$^1/_2$ tsp
Chilli powder	$^3/_4$ Tbsp

1. In a dry wok, dry-fry white sesame seeds over low heat until fragrant and starting to brown. Turn off heat but keep stirring for another 2 minutes. (Black sesame seeds are usually not toasted.) Pound in a mortar and pestle to break up seeds and release oils.
2. Use a sharp knife to cut off thin layers of the zest from mandarin orange peel. Chop very finely.
3. Mix all ingredients together and store in a bottle. Refrigerate to extend shelf life.

Korean Sesame Salt

Makes about 1/2 cup

Like cut chillies and light soy sauce in Chinese noodles or chilli flakes in Indo-Chinese food, Korean and Japanese noodle dishes are often sprinkled with sesame salt. Bottled sesame salt is found in Asian stores but home-made is easy and tastes more fragrant. It keeps well in the fridge. Change the ratio of sesame seeds and salt to suit your taste.

White sesame seeds	1/2 cup
Fine salt	1/2 tsp

1. In a dry wok, dry-fry sesame seeds over low heat until just fragrant and starting to brown. Turn off heat immediately and continue stirring for another 2 minutes.
2. Cool, then pound sesame seeds with salt in a mortar and pestle to get a very coarse powder.
3. Bottle and store in the fridge to extend shelf life.

Toasted Red Chilli Flakes

Makes about 1/2 cup

Toasted chilli flakes is easily available in supermarkets. It is a convenient condiment for beefing up spice levels in most Asian dishes be it salads, noodles or rice, and especially if the dish has to cater to different taste buds. Make your own chilli flakes if you find commercial chilli flakes too seedy or if it is unavailable.

Dried red chillies	50 g (1 2/3 oz), seeded and cut up coarsely

1. Dry-fry chillies in a wok for about 2 minutes over low heat, taking care not to burn chillies.
2. Scoop out and grind in a spice mill if available. The chillies should be in flakes, not powder. If no spice mill is available, process in a food processor by pulsing to as fine as it will get. It does not matter if there are some large pieces. Cut these with a pair of scissors.
3. Bottle in a condiment bottle.

Cucumber Raita

This is the quick way to add some fresh vegetables and protein to a meal. Increase the quantities as needed.

Sliced cucumber	1/2 cup
Yoghurt with or without garlic (page 19)	2 Tbsp
Salt	a pinch
Indian garam masala (page 12)	a pinch

1. Place sliced cucumber on a plate. Spoon yoghurt on top. If using plain yoghurt, sprinkle a pinch of salt and garam masala on it.
2. Serve with any pilaf or flavoured rice.

Garlic Yoghurt Dressing

Makes about 1 cup

Both this dressing and the yoghurt dip (page 19) keep well in the fridge and make an excellent instant dressing for salads, lightly blanched vegetables and flavoured rice. You can ring changes in the flavour with a freshly chopped herb.

Yoghurt	250 g (9 oz)
Garlic	3 cloves, peeled and mashed
Olive oil	1/2 Tbsp
Salt	1 tsp

1. Stir together all ingredients in a glass jar and store in the fridge until required.
2. This yoghurt dressing keeps for at least a week in the fridge.
3. Mix in or sprinkle fresh chopped herb of choice on salad after dressing.

VARY THE FLAVOUR WITH DIFFERENT HERBS:

- Mint
- Parsley
- Flat-leaf parsley
- Dill/dill seeds
- Coriander leaves

Garlic / Onion Yoghurt Dip

Makes about 2 cups

Yoghurt	500 g (1 lb)
Salt	1$\frac{1}{2}$ tsp
Garlic	3 cloves, peeled and finely mashed, or 50 g (1$\frac{2}{3}$ oz) onion, finely chopped and pounded for juice

1. Combine all ingredients together and pour it into a muslin bag. Suspend over kitchen sink overnight to drain whey and get a stiff yoghurt cheese known as *labna*.
2. Store in a glass container in the fridge. It will keep for several weeks.
3. The *labna* can also be diluted into a dressing with some milk and olive oil. Adjust salt to taste.
4. For a different flavour, *labna* can also be flavoured with a chopped herb like coriander, parsley or finely chopped spring onions.
5. Use *labna* with vegetable sticks.

Cooked Yoghurt Sauce

Makes about 2$\frac{1}{2}$ cups

Do not over-boil yoghurt or it will separate. The sauce can be kept plain or flavoured with stock and garlic, onion or a herb like parsley or coriander leaves.

Olive oil	$\frac{1}{2}$ Tbsp
Finely chopped garlic/onion	$\frac{1}{2}$ Tbsp
Stock/milk	250 ml (8 fl oz / 1 cup)
Salt	1 tsp
Yoghurt	250 g (9 oz)

1. Heat olive oil and fry garlic/onion until soft and fragrant.
2. Add stock or milk and salt and bring to a near-boil. Once bubbles appear, whip in yoghurt and continue heating until bubbles appear and sauce begins to bubble up. Turn off heat immediately.
3. Serve with pilafs, biryanis and flavoured rice dishes.

Boiled Prawns

A kilo of fresh prawns in the freezer is a handy standby for many one-dish meals. If prawns are in their shells, boil them as they are and shell after they are cooked. Boiling prawns in their shells keeps them juicy. Prawns are more decorative if their tails are kept on. For some uses such as in fried rice, shell completely. To boil prawns, bring a pot of water to the boil and drop rinsed prawns in their shells into the boiling water. When prawns change colour, they are done. Shell prawns and keep shells for stock.

Prawn Stock

More than half the weight of the prawns is in the head and shells. Thus, 100 g (3^1/$_2$ oz) prawns with head and shell will yield about 50 g (1^2/$_3$ oz) peeled prawns, enough for one serving. Keep the shells and heads for boiling into stock. If insufficient, freeze trimmings until there are at least 4 cups of shells and heads. Combine with 1 litre (32 fl oz / 4 cups) water and boil for 10 minutes. Cool and freeze the prawn stock in small containers and use as a flavouring in other dishes such as fried noodles or in soup. Because the flavour is strong, use in small quantities so as not to overpower other ingredients.

Chicken Stock

Makes about 4 litres (128 fl oz / 16 cups)

Chicken bones, backs, feet	2 kg (4 lb 6 oz)
Water	5 litres (160 fl oz / 20 cups)

1. Put chicken bones and water into a large stock pot and simmer for about 45 minutes.
2. Leave to cool, then skim off as much fat as possible.
3. Ladle stock over a sieve into 1-litre (32-fl oz / 4-cup) boxes, and freeze until needed.

Pork Stock

Makes about 4 litres (128 fl oz / 16 cups)

This takes about 2 hours of simmering. The quick way to do stocks is in a pressure cooker.

Pork bones with meat	2 kg (4 lb 6 oz)
Water	6 litres (192 fl oz / 24 cups)

1. Put pork bones and water into a large stock pot and bring to the boil. Skim off scum that floats to the top during boiling.
2. Simmer gently for 2 hours or until stock is reduced to about 4 litres (128 fl oz / 16 cups).
3. Leave to cool. When bones and meat are cool enough to handle, discard bones but keep meat. Ladle stock over a sieve to remove any bone fragments from stock.
4. Store in 1-litre (32-fl oz / 4-cup) boxes and freeze until needed.

Beef Stock

Makes about 4 litres (128 fl oz / 16 cups)

Beef bones with some meat	2 kg (4 lb 6 oz)
Water	6 litres (192 fl oz / 24 cups)

1. Rinse and put bones and ribs with water in a large stockpot and bring to the boil. Skim off scum that floats to the top during boiling.
2. Simmer over low heat for 3 hours or until liquid is reduced to about 4 litres (128 fl oz / 16 cups). Leave to cool, then skim off as much fat as possible.
3. Ladle stock over a sieve into 1-litre (32-fl oz / 4-cup) boxes, and freeze until needed.

Chinese-style Red Roast Pork / Chicken

Serves 4–8

Chinese-style red roast pork is easily available in wet markets and supermarkets and even in large Asian stores outside Asia. It goes well in Asian salads, fried rice and noodles. Leftovers keep well. Pork can be substituted with chicken if preferred. If care is taken not to over-grill, the meat will stay reasonably juicy. If freshly prepared and kept juicy, it makes a good side dish.

Pork, preferably with some fat	500 g (1 lb 1^1/$_2$ oz)
Red food colouring	a few drops
Sugar/ honey	2 tsp
Dark soy sauce	1 Tbsp
Light soy sauce	^{1}/$_2$ Tbsp

1. Cut pork into thick strips about 5 cm (2 in) across and about 3-cm (1^1/$_4$-in) thick.
2. Mix all ingredients with pork and marinate overnight or for a couple of hours at least.
3. Using medium heat, grill pork on both sides until done, about 15 minutes each side. The length of time depends on the thickness of the meat.

Grilled Chicken, Chinese-style

Serves 4–6

Whatever the style, grilled chicken always makes a good side dish. Barbecue, roast or grill the chicken. Chicken parts cook faster than a whole chicken. If grilling chicken breast, split the breast into two. Gash the thickest part of the chicken breast and smear some seasoning into the meat. Do this also for drumsticks and thighs that are thick. The gashes will help speed up the cooking too. The same seasoning can be used for roasting a whole chicken.

Chicken parts	1 kg (2 lb 3 oz)
Light soy sauce	2 Tbsp
Dark soy sauce	1 tsp
Salt	1 tsp
Sugar/honey	1 Tbsp
Ground white pepper	1 tsp

1. Place chicken in a bowl and add seasoning. Mix well and cover. Leave chicken to marinate in the fridge for several hours or overnight.

Salted Grilled Chicken

Serves 1

This simple dish goes well with salads, fried rice or noodles. The trick is to season the chicken for at least 24 hours before grilling.

Chicken drumstick and thigh	1 per person
Salt	$1^1/_2$ tsp per piece

1. Rub chicken with salt, then cover and refrigerate for 24 hours.
2. Grill for 20–25 minutes until done. The cooking time will depend on the size of the part. Gashing also speeds up the cooking time.

Chinese-style Chicken Vegetable Soup

Serves 1

Pick leafy vegetables like bok choy, cabbage, mustard greens or spinach. Add an extra 125 ml (4 fl oz / $^1/_2$ cup) stock for boiling the soup. Make this soup with either pork or chicken stock.

Chicken stock (page 20)	125–180 ml (4–6 fl oz / $^1/_2$–$^3/_4$ cup)
Salt	to taste
Leafy vegetables	150 g ($5^1/_3$ oz) per person
Sliced carrots	2–3 slices per serving
Fried garlic/fried shallots (page 11)	1 tsp per serving
Garlic/shallot oil (page 11)	1 tsp per serving

1. Heat chicken stock with salt to taste and when it boils up, add vegetables. Simmer until vegetables are cooked to preferred texture.
2. Just before serving, stir in fried garlic/shallots and garlic/shallot oil.

Chinese-style Stir-fried Vegetables

Serves 4–5

The amount of vegetable used would depend on the type of vegetable. Estimate 500 g (1 lb 1 1/2 oz) or about two small heads of broccoli for 4–5 people. For leafy vegetables like spinach, estimate 1 kg (2 lb 3 oz) for trimming and shrinkage. For mixed frozen vegetables, estimate about 1/2 cup per person.

Cooking oil	1 Tbsp
Garlic	1 clove, peeled and chopped
Salt	1/2 tsp
Vegetables of choice	as needed
Light soy sauce	1 Tbsp

1. Heat oil in a wok and stir-fry garlic until fragrant.
2. Add salt, stir, then add vegetables and light soy sauce. For firm vegetables, add a couple of tablespoonfuls of water or stock.
3. Turn off heat when vegetables change colour. Dish out and serve.

Blanched Vegetables with Oil Dressing

Serves 4–5

Many vegetables are tasty if simply steamed or blanched and dressed with some garlic or shallot oil (page 11) or sesame oil and light soy sauce. Steaming is preferable as the nutrients are not leached out in the boiling water.

Vegetables of choice	as needed
Garlic oil/shallot oil/sesame oil	to taste
Salt/light soy sauce	to taste

1. Either steam the cleaned and cut vegetables in a steamer or blanch them for 10–20 seconds in boiling water depending on the vegetable and preference.
2. Scoop vegetables using a wire scoop and drain well. Place on a serving plate.
3. Drizzle oil of choice and light soy sauce over vegetables. Toss if preferred.

Pickled Vegetables

This pickling mix can be used with firm ingredients like shallots, garlic, green beans, long beans and cauliflower. Shallots and garlic take longer to pickle than vegetables. This pickle keeps well without refrigeration and can be chopped up and added to spike the flavour of salads, noodles and fried rice. The pickling mix can be used to pickle between 300 g (11 oz) and 500 g (1 lb 1½ oz) ingredients if they are kept pressed down.

VEGETABLES

- Green beans
- Long beans
- Cabbage
- Cauliflower
- Radish
- Carrots
- Daikon
- Tientsin cabbage
- Mustard cabbage
- Garlic
- Small onions
- Shallots
- Green chillies
- Young ginger

PICKLING MIX

Chinese white rice vinegar	500 ml (16 fl oz / 2 cups)
Sugar	250 g (9 oz)
Salt	1½ tsp

1. Combine pickling mix ingredients in a stainless steel saucepan and bring to the boil. Simmer until sugar and salt have dissolved. Leave to cool.
2. The vegetables for pickling should be cleaned, cut into bite-size pieces and blanched for 10 seconds in boiling water. Cool before stirring into pickling mix.
3. Bottle and store in a cool place until needed. Stand overnight before serving.

The Taste Test

Every cook has different preferences for sweet, sour and salty. Ingredients also vary in how sweet, salty or sour they are. Accuracy in something so changeable as taste is hard. The only way is to taste as you go along and adjust the taste to suit yourself and those whom you are cooking for. Deciding whether an ingredient is cooked also requires guesswork because the size of the meat, seafood and/or vegetables affect cooking. With some ingredients such as prawns, fish or squid, undercooking is better than overcooking and most residual heat is enough to finish the cooking. Do the taste test to double-check.

Preparation Time Versus Cooking Time

It is difficult to estimate preparation time as many of the ingredients that I use are usually prepared way ahead of time and are sitting in the fridge. Some cooks are also faster while some have more appliances on hand. Therefore, the preparation times are at best estimates based on the ready availability of certain key ingredients.

Terminology

Aubergines:	Eggplants, brinjals
Adzuki beans:	Red beans
Capsicum:	Bell pepper
Chickpeas:	Garbanzo beans
Cooking oil:	Unless specified, oil means a neutral cooking oil like canola, corn or soy bean oil
Coriander leaves:	Cilantro
Cornflour:	Cornstarch
Cup:	The standard metric measuring cup. Each standard measuring cup of uncooked rice weighs 200 g (7 oz) while each rice cooker cup of uncooked rice weighs approximately 150 g ($5^1/_3$ oz). All cup measures are level.
Fermented soy beans:	*Taucheo*, medium-brown miso
Ghee:	Clarified butter and available in tins
Mirin:	Japanese sweet cooking wine
Packed cup:	Press herbs into cup
Parsley:	Flat-leaf and curly parsley are interchangeable
Prawns:	Shrimps
Rice cooker cup:	The plastic cup that comes with a rice cooker and used for measuring rice and water. The size is practically the same across different brands of rice cookers. Each rice cooker cup of uncooked rice weighs about 150 g ($5^1/_3$ oz). *See also* Cup.
Spring onions:	Green onions, scallions
Yam bean:	Jicama, *bangkuang*

Everyday One-dish Meals

One-dish meals simplify preparation and presentation.
They taste great eaten hot around a dining table,
carried to a pot luck meal, or cold at a picnic.

Fried Glass Noodles with Pork, Cantonese-style

Preparation time: 45 minutes   Serves 3–4

Although the list of ingredients looks long, this dish does not take long to put together. Once all the essentials are assembled ready for the wok, it takes just minutes to fry it up.

Cooking oil	2 Tbsp
Chopped garlic	1 tsp
Ginger	4 slices, finely shredded
Leeks	200 g (7 oz), thinly sliced
Glass noodles	300 g (11 oz), softened in cold water
Spring onion	1, small, finely chopped
Red chilli-vinegar sauce (page 15)	

PORK AND MARINADE

Pork	150 g (5$^1/_3$ oz), cut into matchsticks
Dark soy sauce	$^1/_2$ tsp
Light soy sauce	2 tsp
Cornflour	1 tsp
Water	1 tsp
Sesame oil	1 tsp
Ground white pepper	a pinch

SAUCE

Chicken stock (page 20)	250 ml (8 fl oz / 1 cup)
Chinese rice wine	2 tsp
Salt	1 tsp
Sesame oil	2 tsp
Light soy sauce	2 Tbsp

1. Marinate pork and set aside for 10 minutes.
2. Mix together sauce ingredients and set aside.
3. Heat oil in a wok and sauté garlic and ginger until fragrant.
4. Stir in pork and fry for 1 minute before adding leeks and sauce mixture. Bring to the boil.
5. Add noodles and simmer for 5 minutes or until liquid has been mostly absorbed into noodles. It should still be slightly moist.
6. Stir in chopped spring onions. Serve hot with a condiment such as red chilli-vinegar sauce.

Yam Woon Sen (Thai Glass Noodle Salad)

Preparation time: 45 minutes   Serves 3–4

This best known of Thai salads makes an excellent one-dish meal if the dressing is kept fairly light. Although usually eaten with rice, it actually has everything in it to make a complete meal. Substitute the freshly boiled seafood with a piece of boiled pork or chicken, or minced meat.

Coriander leaves	2 large bunches with root
Glass noodles	400 g (14$^{1}/_{3}$ oz), softened in cold water
Wood ear fungus	$^{1}/_{4}$ cup, softened in cold water
Indo-Chinese dressing (page 15)	125 ml (4 fl oz / $^{1}/_{2}$ cup)
Small-medium prawns	200 g (7 oz), boiled and peeled
Small squid or squid rings	100 g (3$^{1}/_{2}$ oz), boiled lightly
Tomato	50 g (1$^{2}/_{3}$ oz)
Romaine lettuce	100 g (3$^{1}/_{2}$ oz), shredded
Shallots	50 g (1$^{2}/_{3}$ oz), peeled and thinly sliced
Spring onion	1, chopped
Basil (optional)	$^{1}/_{2}$ cup
Mint (optional)	$^{1}/_{2}$ cup

1. Prepare coriander before cooking glass noodles and wood ear fungus. Trim roots, rinse clean and pound roots to mush. Squeeze juice into a large bowl and set aside. Chop up coriander leaves and set aside.

2. Bring a pot of water to the boil and cook glass noodles for 3 minutes. Scoop out with a wire sieve and drain well. Keep water on the boil. Stir glass noodles into coriander juice.

3. If wood ear fungus is very big, slice into strips. Discard hard stem. Blanch in boiling water for 2 minutes. Scoop out and add to glass noodles.

4. Stir Indo-Chinese dressing into glass noodles and adjust seasoning to taste. Add remaining ingredients.

5. Serve immediately.

Korean Sweet Potato Noodles with Beef and Mixed Vegetables

Preparation time: 45 minutes   Serves 3–4

While this is usually a Korean side dish to be eaten with rice, it actually makes a good one-dish meal. For a truly Korean flavour, stir in a tablespoon of raw chopped garlic after the noodles are cooked. If sweet potato noodles are not available, substitute with glass or tapioca noodles. Sweet potato noodles do not sit well.

Beef	300 g (11 oz), cut into matchsticks
Cooking oil	2 Tbsp
Onion	50 g ($1^2/_3$ oz), peeled and thinly sliced
Carrots	150 g ($5^1/_3$ oz), peeled and sliced
Dried shiitake mushrooms	3–4, large, softened in cold water and sliced
Leeks	150 g ($5^1/_3$ oz), halved and slant-cut into 2-cm ($^3/_4$-in) lengths
Watercress	150 g ($5^1/_3$ oz), cut into 2-cm lengths
Sweet potato noodles	300 g (11 oz), softened in cold water
Salt	$^1/_2$ tsp
Sugar	2 tsp
Light soy sauce	1 Tbsp
Chicken stock (page 20)	250 ml (8 fl oz / 1 cup)

MARINADE

Bicarbonate of soda	a pinch
Sugar	3 tsp
Chopped garlic	1 Tbsp
Chopped spring onion	1 Tbsp
Sesame oil	$1^1/_2$ Tbsp
Dark soy sauce	1 tsp
Light soy sauce	1 Tbsp
Ground black pepper	$^1/_2$ tsp

CONDIMENTS (OPTIONAL)

Kimchi

Vinegar-chilli dip (page 16)

Chopped, slivered or whole raw garlic

1. Combine marinade ingredients and add beef. Set aside for 10 minutes.
2. Heat 1 Tbsp oil in a wok and sauté beef for 1–2 minutes. Dish out and set aside.
3. Add remaining 1 Tbsp oil to wok and sauté onion, carrot, mushrooms and leeks for 2–3 minutes. Add watercress, noodles, salt, sugar and soy sauce. Mix well.
4. Add chicken stock and continue frying until noodles have absorbed stock. Stir cooked beef into noodles. Dish out and serve with a condiment.

Hamhung Nyaeng Myon

(Dressed Sweet Potato Noodles, Hamhung-style)

Preparation time: 30 minutes   Serves 3–4

This spicy version of *nyaeng myon* is also called *bibim nyaeng myon*. Try making this dish after you have just made Pyongyang *nyaeng myon* (page 80) because you should have some boiled beef and Korean pear on hand. Turn the broth that goes into Pyongyang *nyaeng myon* into a soup to go with this dry noodle dish. Hamhung is in North Korea from where this dish is said to have originated. The dressing for the noodles makes a single dressing. Repeat as necessary.

Sweet potato noodles	300 g (11 oz), softened in cold water
Boiled beef brisket	200 g (7 oz), thinly sliced
Korean pear	4 slices
Egg	2, hard-boiled, peeled and halved
Cucumber	1, cored, cut into thin slivers
Kimchi	1/2 cup
Korean sesame salt (page 17) or *shichimi togarashi* (page 16)	to taste

DRESSING FOR NOODLES (SERVES 1)

Garlic	1 clove, peeled and finely pounded
Ginger	1 slice, finely pounded
Red chillies	2, seeded and pounded to a paste
Sesame oil	1 Tbsp
Honey	2 tsp
Light soy sauce	1 Tbsp
Kimchi juice	1 Tbsp

1. Prepare dressing. Pound garlic, ginger and chillies to a fine paste. Mix with the other ingredients in a deep-dish plate. Repeat for the number of servings.

2. Bring a pot of water to the boil and blanch noodles until tender but still al dente or about 3 minutes. Drain well and divide noodles into the number of servings as required and stir into dressing. Twirl noodles into a heap in the centre of the plate.

3. Garnish with sliced beef, pear, egg, cucumber and kimchi.

4. Serve with a small bowl of beef broth on the side. The broth can also be emptied into the noodles. Serve with Korean sesame salt.

Glass Noodles with Minced Meat

Preparation time: 45 minutes   Serves 3–4

Adapt this noodle dish to whatever vegetables or meat that are on hand. You could even just go with mushrooms and dried prawns which are common in many South East Asian larders. The condiment will give it plenty of zing.

Cooking oil	3 Tbsp
Chopped garlic	1 Tbsp
Dried prawns	1 Tbsp, cleaned and chopped finely
Dried shiitake mushrooms	4, softened in cold water and thinly sliced
Minced pork/chicken	100 g (3$^{1}/_{2}$ oz)
Leeks	200 g (7 oz), thinly sliced
Glass noodles	300 g (11 oz), softened in cold water
Water or chicken stock (page 20)	250 ml (8 fl oz / 1 cup)
Dark soy sauce	1 tsp
Light soy sauce	2 Tbsp
Salt	$^{1}/_{2}$ tsp

CONDIMENTS (OPTIONAL)

Red chillies with soy sauce (page 15)

Sambal belacan with lime juice (page 13)

Pickled green chillies (page 25)

1. Heat oil in a wok and sauté garlic until fragrant.
2. Add dried prawns and sauté for 1 minute, then stir in mushrooms, minced pork/chicken and leeks. Mix well.
3. Stir in glass noodles, water or chicken stock, soy sauces and salt. Mix well and simmer over low heat for 3 minutes or until noodle are tender.
4. Serve hot with a condiment.

Fried Glass Noodles, Filipino-style

Preparation time: 45 minutes   Serves 3–4

The Filipinos call glass noodles *sotanghoon* and what makes this different from the Cantonese-style glass noodles is the calamansi lime juice as well as the annatto oil. This coloured oil is made by cooking a tablespoon of annatto seeds in 125 ml (4 fl oz / ¹⁄₂ cup) oil. The seeds turn the oil red and annatto oil adds colour to the transparent noodles without the spiciness of chillies. The use of lard also gives these glass noodles a different flavour and mouthfeel.

Cooking oil/annatto oil/lard	3 Tbsp
Chopped onion	2 Tbsp
Chopped garlic	1 Tbsp
Dried shiitake mushrooms	3–4, softened in cold water and thinly sliced; water reserved for sauce
Chicken	200 g (7 oz), thinly sliced
Carrots	150 g (5¹⁄₃ oz), peeled and cut into matchsticks
Leeks	150 g (5¹⁄₃ oz), cut into 2-cm (³⁄₄-cm) lengths
Glass noodles	300 g (11 oz), softened in cold water
Fish sauce	3 Tbsp
Lime juice	1 Tbsp

SAUCE

Mushroom water	4 Tbsp
Chicken stock (page 20)	125 ml (4 fl oz / ¹⁄₂ cup)
Bay leaves	2, crushed
Fish sauce	2 Tbsp
Salt	¹⁄₂ tsp

CONDIMENTS (OPTIONAL)

Red chilli-vinegar sauce (page 15)

Red chillies with fish sauce (page 15)

Vinegar-chilli dip (page 16)

1. Combine water from soaking mushrooms with chicken stock, bay leaves, fish sauce and salt and boil mixture for 2 minutes. Discard bay leaves and set aside.
2. Heat oil in a wok and fry chopped onion and garlic until onion is soft. Stir in mushrooms, chicken and sauce mixture. Bring to the boil.
3. Add carrots and leeks and fry until leeks change colour.
4. Stir in glass noodles and fish sauce and simmer for 3 minutes. The noodles should be moist rather than dry. Add a little more water if necessary.
5. Turn off heat and stir in lime juice.
6. Serve hot with a condiment.

Glass Noodles with Chinese Stewed Pork

Preparation time: 30 minutes   Serves 3–4

This is my emergency one-dish meal and the reason for that can of Chinese stewed pork in my larder. This dish does not have "canned food" written all over it even though three of the major ingredients are from the larder. It is equally tasty with dried rice vermicelli substituted for glass noodles.

Premium Chinese stewed pork	1 can (256 g / 9 oz)
Lard from stewed pork	2 Tbsp
Dark soy sauce	1 tsp
Light soy sauce	2 Tbsp
Salt	$1/2$ tsp
Water or chicken or pork stock (pages 20 and 21)	500 ml (16 fl oz / 2 cups)
Chopped garlic	1 Tbsp
Red chillies	3–4, seeded and coarsely sliced
Dried shiitake mushrooms	4, softened in cold water and sliced
Glass noodles	300 g (11 oz), softened in cold water
Mustard greens	300 g (11 oz), cut into finger lengths

1. Open can of stewed pork and chill in the fridge or freezer to get fat to harden. Lift lard up and use it for frying.
2. Pour out stewed pork into a large bowl and pick out skin and bones, leaving just lean meat and gravy. There won't be much. Add soy sauces, salt and water or stock to gravy and meat.
3. Heat lard in a wok and sauté chopped garlic, chillies and mushrooms until fragrant.
4. Add lean stewed pork and gravy mixture and glass noodles and bring to the boil. Simmer over low heat for about 3 minutes before adding vegetables. Stir-fry until vegetables change colour.
5. Serve hot.

Fried Rice Vermicelli with Fish Sauce and Lime Juice

Preparation time: 45 minutes   Serves 3–4

This is Thai-style fried rice vermicelli with the sugar, toasted chilli flakes and peanuts as optionals. If possible, use bird's eye chillies so that the noodles have some bite.

Cooking oil	4 Tbsp
Chopped garlic	1 Tbsp
Peeled prawns	100 g (3$\frac{1}{2}$ oz)
Fish cake	200 g (7 oz), sliced into strips
Red chillies	3–4, seeded and cut into strips
Bean sprouts	250 g (9 oz), tailed
Carrot	100 g (3$\frac{1}{2}$ oz), peeled and julienned
Dried thin/medium rice vermicelli	300 g (11 oz), softened in cold water
Fish sauce	4 Tbsp
Chives	1 bundle, cut into finger lengths

GARNISH
Lime halves
Chopped toasted peanuts
  (page 10)
Toasted red chilli flakes (page 17)
Fine granulated sugar

1. Heat oil in a wok and sauté garlic until fragrant and pale yellow.
2. Add prawns and fish cake followed by chillies, bean sprouts, carrot and rice vermicelli. Stir well, then add fish sauce and chives and fry until noodles are tender but al dente. Sprinkle in some water if necessary.
3. Serve noodles garnished with lime halves, chopped peanuts, sugar and chilli flakes to taste.

Noodles in Miso Soup with Salmon

Preparation time: 45 minutes   Serves 3–4

Make miso soup just before serving as the flavour deteriorates if the soup is left standing. Make this soup out of frozen chicken stock. For more convenience, use bottled dashi soup concentrate available in Japanese supermarkets. Dilute it more than as instructed. The salmon can be substituted with soft bean curd, chicken, pork or prawns. Chrysanthemum leaves can also be substituted with another vegetable that cooks quickly such as baby spinach.

Udon/soba/somen	300 g (11 oz)
White miso	3 Tbsp
Chicken stock (page 20)	1 litre (32 fl oz / 4 cups)
Salmon	200 g (7 oz), sliced
Chrysanthemum leaves	200 g (7 oz)
Freshly grated ginger	1 tsp
Spring onion	1, finely shredded
Shredded nori	a handful
Shichimi togarashi (page 16)	

1. Cook noodles before making miso soup. Divide into serving bowls.
2. Dissolve miso in a small quantity of stock. Set aside.
3. To make miso soup, bring stock to the boil. Add salmon and boil for 1–2 minutes, depending on the size of the pieces. Add chrysanthemum leaves and miso and return to the boil. Turn off heat. Stir in freshly grated ginger.
4. Ladle hot miso soup over noodles and top with spring onion and nori shreds.
5. Serve immediately with *shichimi togarashi*.

RINGING CHANGES

To ring subtle changes in flavour, make miso soup with different stocks such as plain konbu or shiitake and experiment with different combinations of seafood, meat and vegetables. Some combinations taste and look better than others. Note that the appearance of a dish is very important in Japanese cuisine.

- Prawns and shiso leaves
- Salmon and bean curd
- Japanese fish cake (*kamaboko*) and leeks
- Crabstick and aubergine
- Soft bean curd and shiso leaves
- Stuffed soy bean puffs (*inari*) and carrots
- Chrysanthemum leaves and chicken or pork
- Fresh mushrooms and prawns, salmon or chicken
- Fresh or dried mushrooms with assorted vegetables

Fried Soy Bean Noodles with Bean Curd and Leeks

Preparation time: 45 minutes   Serves 3–4

Soy bean noodles come labelled somewhat vaguely as "bean noodles". Made with soy bean flour, bean noodles are high in protein and have a good bite. These wide-cut dried noodles make good leftovers as they do not get mushy although you should not over-boil them. So be ready to add the noodles to the other ingredients once you have got a pot of water on the boil.

Soy bean noodles	300 g (11 oz)
Cooking oil	4 Tbsp
Chopped garlic	1 Tbsp
Dried shiitake mushrooms	4–5, softened in cold water and thinly sliced
Minced pork/chicken	50 g (1^2/$_3$ oz)
Peeled prawns	100 g (3^1/$_2$ oz), deveined
Leeks	150 g (5^1/$_3$ oz), sliced thinly
Firm bean curd	100 g (3^1/$_2$ oz), cut into chunky short strips
Dark soy sauce	1 tsp
Light soy sauce	2 Tbsp
Salt	^{1}/$_2$ tsp
Water or chicken stock (page 20)	125 ml (4 fl oz / ^{1}/$_2$ cup)

CONDIMENTS (OPTIONAL)

Red chillies with soy sauce (page 15)

Sambal belacan with lime juice (page 13)

Pickled green chillies (page 25)

Red chilli-vinegar sauce (page 15)

1. Prepare ingredients for frying before starting to boil noodles.
2. Bring a pot of salted water to the boil, add noodles and while noodles are boiling, start frying other ingredients.
3. In a wok, heat oil and sauté garlic until fragrant.
4. Add mushrooms, pork/chicken, mix well, then add prawns, leeks and bean curd. Sauté until leeks change colour.
5. Scoop out nearly-cooked noodles from pot of boiling water and add to the wok. The noodles should still be undercooked and very al dente.
6. Add soy sauces, salt and water or chicken stock to the wok and fry for 1–2 minutes until noodles are tender.
7. Serve hot with a condiment.

Vegetarian Rice Vermicelli, Indian-style

Preparation time: 45 minutes   Serves 3–4

This dish of fried noodles makes good picnic food even in hot weather as there is no worry about meat spoiling. Ring changes in the type of noodles by substituting rice vermicelli with dried wheat noodles.

Cooking oil	4 Tbsp
Onion	50 g (1^2/$_3$ oz), peeled and thinly sliced
Chopped garlic	1 Tbsp
Ginger	6 slices, finely chopped
Cooked dried red chilli paste (page 14)	1 Tbsp
Tomato	100 g (3^1/$_2$ oz), cubed
Salt	1^1/$_2$ tsp
Firm bean curd	100 g (3^1/$_2$ oz), cubed
Cabbage	100 g (3^1/$_2$ oz), shredded
Mustard greens	100 g (3^1/$_2$ oz), cut into finger lengths
Peas	50 g (1^2/$_3$ oz / ^{1}/$_4$ cup)
Bean sprouts	100 g (3^1/$_2$ oz)
Dried thin rice vermicelli	300 g (11 oz), softened in cold water
Spring onion	1, chopped
Indian garam masala (optional)	^{1}/$_4$ tsp

CONDIMENTS (OPTIONAL)
Pickled green chillies (page 25)
Chutney
Lime/lemon wedges
Toasted red chilli flakes (page 17)

1. Heat oil in a wok and sauté onion, garlic and ginger until fragrant but not brown. Add chilli paste and fry until oil surfaces. Add tomato and salt and cook until tomato is soft.
2. Stir in bean curd, cabbage, mustard greens and peas and sauté until mustard greens start to change colour.
3. Add bean sprouts and noodles and mix well. Fry until noodles are tender but still al dente. Lastly, stir in chopped spring onion. If using garam masala, sprinkle a little in and mix well.
4. Serve hot or cold with a condiment of choice.

Spicy Rice Vermicelli with Herbs

Preparation time: 45 minutes   Serves 3–4

Fresh herbs give this fried rice vermicelli its great flavour. Use whatever fresh herbs you have on hand. At a pinch, you can substitute with dried herbs but use just one kind as dried herbs are stronger in flavour than fresh herbs. The easiest combination would be coriander leaves and spring onions. Basil, mint and saw-tooth herb will give this dish a Thai or Vietnamese flavour.

Cooking oil	4 Tbsp
Chopped garlic	1 Tbsp
Fish cake	100 g (3^1/$_2$ oz), sliced into strips
Peeled prawns	100 g (3^1/$_2$ oz), deveined
Light soy sauce	2 Tbsp
Bean sprouts	300 g (11 oz), tailed
Salt	1 tsp
Dried thin/medium rice vermicelli	300 g (11 oz), softened in cold water until pliable
Mix of herbs (coriander leaves, spring onion, Chinese celery, turmeric leaves, basil, mint)	2 cups, chopped

SPICE PASTE

Red chillies	50 g (1^2/$_3$ oz), seeded
Shallots	50 g (1^2/$_3$ oz), peeled
Garlic	2 cloves, peeled
Water	1 Tbsp

GARNISH

Lime halves

1. Prepare spice paste first. Put all spice paste ingredients into a food processor and blend until fine.
2. Heat 1 Tbsp oil in a wok and sauté garlic until fragrant and pale gold. Add fish cake, prawns, 1 Tbsp light soy sauce, and stir-fry until prawns change colour. The mixture should be moist. Dish out and set aside.
3. Heat remaining oil in the wok and fry spice paste until oil surfaces.
4. Add bean sprouts, salt and remaining light soy sauce and mix well. Stir in rice vermicelli and fry until noodles are nearly tender.
5. Stir in cooked fish cake and prawn mixture and mix well. Continue frying until noodles are tender.
6. Add chopped herbs last, mixing well into the noodles. Turn off heat when herbs turn limp.
7. Serve hot or cold garnished with lime halves.

Vegetarian Rice Vermicelli with Five-spice Powder

Preparation time: 45 minutes   Serves 3–4

In traditional Chinese vegetarian food, there is no garlic or onions in the seasoning as these bulbs are considered to be stimulating and therefore inappropriate for vegetarians who are presumed to be trying to tame their wilder emotions. Note that Chinese five-spice powder can vary greatly in fragrance. Adjust to taste. Substitute rice noodles with thin dried wheat noodles if preferred. If bean curd sticks are unavailable, substitute with a large square of firm bean curd which should first be browned in some oil before it is cut into bite-size pieces.

Cooking oil	4 Tbsp
Chopped garlic	1 Tbsp
Water	250 ml (8 fl oz / 1 cup)
Dry shiitake mushrooms	2–3, softened in cold water and sliced
Dried bean curd sticks	2–3 pieces, softened in cold water and cut into finger lengths
Chinese five-spice powder	$^1/_2$ tsp
Dark soy sauce	2 tsp
Light soy sauce	2 Tbsp
Salt	$1^1/_2$ tsp
Cabbage	250 g (9 oz), shredded
Carrot	100 g ($3^1/_2$ oz), peeled and julienned
Dried thin/medium rice vermicelli	300 g (11 oz), softened in cold water

CONDIMENTS (OPTIONAL)
Pickled green chillies (page 25)
Red chillies with soy sauce (page 15)
Vinegar-chilli dip (page 16)

1. Prepare ingredients before starting to fry.
2. Heat oil, fry garlic until pale gold. Add water, mushrooms, bean curd sticks, five-spice powder, soy sauces and salt and bring to the boil. Turn down heat and simmer until liquid is half gone.
3. Add cabbage and carrot and fry until cabbage turns limp. Adjust seasoning to taste.
4. Stir in softened noodles and mix well. Continue frying for another 5–10 minutes until noodles are tender but al dente.
5. Serve hot or cold with a condiment of choice.

Fried Mouse-tail Noodles with Sichuan Vegetable

Preparation time: 30 minutes   Serves 3–4

Sichuan vegetable is a fleshy vegetable pickled in chilli powder and salt. It is sold in dry goods shops, wet market stalls that sell pickled vegetables or stores that carry Chinese produce. It is pleasantly spicy with a delicious crunch and goes well in soups and in this case, in a stir-fry.

Sichuan vegetable	200 g (7 oz)
Dark soy sauce	1/2 tsp
Light soy sauce	1 Tbsp
Sesame oil	1 tsp
Cornflour	1 tsp
Pork	200 g (7 oz), cut into matchsticks
Cooking oil	4 Tbsp
Chopped garlic	1 Tbsp
Red chilli	1, seeded and thinly sliced
Mouse-tail noodles	500 g (1 lb 1 1/2 oz)
Spring onion	1, small, chopped

SAUCE

Water or chicken stock (page 20)	250 ml (8 fl oz / 1 cup)
Salt	1/4 tsp
Light soy sauce	1 Tbsp
Sesame oil	1 tsp
Cornflour	1/2 Tbsp
Sugar	1 tsp

1. Rinse Sichuan vegetable, slice into matchsticks and soak in several changes of cold water to leach out some of the salt. Do not over leach.

2. Mix soy sauces and sesame oil with cornflour and pork strips. Set aside.

3. Combine ingredients for sauce and set aside.

4. Heat 1 Tbsp oil in a wok and fry marinated pork for 1 minute or until meat changes colour. Dish out and set aside.

5. Heat remaining oil in the same wok and fry garlic until fragrant. Add Sichuan vegetable and chilli and fry for 1 minute. Add noodles and fry for 2 minutes, then add fried pork. Fry for another minute.

6. Stir up sauce mixture before adding to noodles. Bring to the boil.

7. Garnish with chopped spring onion and serve hot.

Fried Mouse-tail Noodles, Thai-style

Preparation time: 30 minutes   Serves 3–4

Fresh mouse-tail noodles fry well even when fried repeatedly. If pulling a noodle out of the larder, substitute fresh mouse-tail noodles with dried flat rice noodles (*guotiao*) or dried coarse rice vermicelli. If substituting with other fresh noodles, use coarse rice vermicelli rather than fresh flat rice noodles (*guotiao*) as it will not stand up well to repeated stirring.

Cooking oil	5 Tbsp
Garlic	4 cloves, peeled and chopped
Shallots	4, peeled and thinly sliced
Fresh mouse-tail noodles	600 g (1 lb 5$\frac{1}{3}$ oz)
Cooked dried red chilli paste (page 14)	1 Tbsp
Pork/chicken/prawns	100 g (3$\frac{1}{2}$ oz / $\frac{1}{2}$ cup), cut pork/chicken into matchsticks, and peel and devein prawns
Firm bean curd	200 g (7 oz), cut into strips
Spring onion	1, cut into finger lengths
Bean sprouts	300 g (11 oz)
Eggs	2

SEASONING

Tamarind paste	2 Tbsp
Water	85 ml (2$\frac{1}{2}$ fl oz / $\frac{1}{3}$ cup)
Sugar	3 Tbsp
Fish sauce	4 Tbsp

GARNISH

Ground roasted peanuts	50 g (1$\frac{2}{3}$ oz / $\frac{1}{4}$ cup)
Lime wedges	
Spring onion	1, chopped
Basil leaves	1 handful
Coriander leaves	1 bunch, chopped

1. Prepare seasoning. Mix tamarind paste with water and strain juice. Discard solids. Mix tamarind juice with sugar and fish sauce. Set aside.

2. Heat 2 Tbsp oil in a wok and fry garlic and shallots until brown. Add noodles and 2 Tbsp seasoning mixture. Fry for 1 minute, a little longer if noodles are rather firm. If necessary, sprinkle a little water over noodles to help soften them. Dish out and set aside.

3. Heat 1 Tbsp oil in the wok and fry chilli paste for 1 minute. Add meat or prawns and fry for another minute. Stir in bean curd and spring onions and three-quarters of bean sprouts. Mix well. Stir in remaining seasoning mixture, fry for 1 minute, then dish out and set aside.

4. Heat last spoonful of oil in wok and add eggs, breaking yolks up and spreading eggs out to set. Return noodles and other fried ingredients to wok and mix well.

5. Turn off heat and stir in remaining bean sprouts. Dish out, garnish and serve immediately.

Spicy Fried Mouse-tail Noodles

Preparation time: 30 minutes   Serves 3–4

Fried mouse-tail noodles makes great picnic food as it is easy to serve and is tasty even at room temperature. Dried rice vermicelli, thin or coarse, is also good fried this way.

Cooking oil	4 Tbsp
Chopped garlic	2 Tbsp
Cooked dried red chilli paste (page 14)	1 Tbsp
Peeled prawns	100 g ($3^1/_2$ oz), deveined
Fish cake	100 g ($3^1/_2$ oz), thinly sliced
Tientsin cabbage	300 g (11 oz), thinly sliced
Mouse-tail noodles	500 g (1 lb $1^1/_2$ oz)
Carrot	50 g ($1^2/_3$ oz), peeled and cut into matchsticks
Light soy sauce	2 Tbsp
Dark soy sauce	1 tsp
Salt	$1/_2$ tsp

CONDIMENT (OPTIONAL)
Vinegar-chilli dip (page 16)

1. Heat oil in a wok and sauté garlic until fragrant. Add chilli paste and fry until oil surfaces. Add prawns and fish cake, then Tientsin cabbage and mix well. Fry until cabbage is limp.

2. When vegetables are limp, stir in noodles, carrot, soy sauces and salt and fry for about 3 minutes or until noodles are tender but still al dente. If noodles start to stick, sprinkle in a couple of spoonfuls of water.

3. Serve hot with vinegar-chilli dip if desired.

Balinese Fried Noodles

Preparation time: 1 hour   Serves 3–4

The hard part about doing these noodles is putting together the spice paste. Double or treble the portions and freeze the spice paste for use another day. Or cheat and substitute with bottled tomato sauce with some pounded lemon grass, bottled *sambal oelek*, ginger and Indonesian sweet dark soy sauce (*kicap manis*) added to it. Bottled *sambal oelek* from Indonesia is easily found in supermarkets and Asian stores abroad.

Fresh wheat noodles	600 g (1 lb 5 oz) or 300 g (11 oz) dried egg noodles
Cooking oil	4 Tbsp
Eggs	3, beaten
Onion	1, peeled and cut into thin rings
Prawns	200 g (7 oz), peeled and deveined
Cabbage	400 g (14$^1/_3$ oz), shredded
Carrot	1, peeled and cut into matchsticks

SPICE PASTE

Ripe tomatoes	100 g (3$^1/_2$ oz)
Cooking oil	125 ml (4 fl oz / $^1/_2$ cup)
Shallots	50 g (1$^2/_3$ oz), peeled and thinly sliced
Garlic	2 cloves, peeled and thinly sliced
Red chillies	100 g (3$^1/_2$ oz), seeded and coarsely chopped
Ginger	4 slices
Lemon grass	1 stalk, finely sliced
Water	4 Tbsp
Sugar	2 tsp
Salt	1 tsp
Indonesian sweet dark soy sauce (*kicap manis*)	1 Tbsp

GARNISH
Fried shallots (page 11)
Lime halves

1. Prepare spice paste. Using a sharp knife, peel tomatoes, then chop coarsely. Heat oil in a saucepan and fry shallots until soft. Add garlic and sauté for 1 minute. Add rest of ingredients and simmer for 3 minutes. Cool mixture, then blend into a thick paste. Return blended paste to the pot and simmer until oil surfaces.

2. Bring a pot of water to the boil and blanch noodles until nearly tender but still very al dente. Drain well and set aside.

3. Heat a bit of oil in a wok and make omelettes of beaten eggs. Cut into thin strips.

4. Heat remaining oil and sauté onion for 1 minute. Add prawns and when they turn pink, add cabbage and carrot and fry for 1 minute.

5. Stir in cooked spice paste and blanched noodles. Fry for 1–2 minutes until noodles are tender but still al dente.

6. Dish out and garnish with fried shallots and lime halves.

Kimchi Soup with Noodles or Rice

Preparation time: 30 minutes   Serves 3–4

Packaged kimchi usually comes with some of the pickling liquid. Do not discard as this tart spicy liquid makes very tasty seasoning for soup. Make kimchi rice or noodle soup with cooked rice or boiled noodles added to it.

Kimchi with liquid	300 ml (10 fl oz / 1¼ cups)
Sesame oil	1 Tbsp
Chopped garlic	2 Tbsp
Fermented soy beans (*taucheo*)	½ Tbsp
Chicken/pork/prawn stock (pages 20–21)	750 ml (24 fl oz / 3 cups)
Chicken/pork/beef/prawns	200 g (7 oz)
Soft bean curd	200 g (7 oz), cubed
Salt (optional)	½ tsp

NOODLES OR RICE

Fresh rice noodles	500 g (1 lb 1½ oz)
Dried wheat or rice noodles	300 g (11 oz)
Cooked rice	3 cups (from 225 g / 8 oz / 1½ rice cooker cups rice)

GARNISH

Chopped coriander leaves	
Chopped spring onions	
Garlic	3 cloves, peeled and cut into chunks or slivers

1. If kimchi is in large pieces, cut into bite-size pieces.
2. Heat sesame oil in a large pot and sauté garlic and fermented soy beans until fragrant. Add stock and kimchi with liquid and bring to the boil.
3. Add meat or prawns or the combination and when meat is cooked, add bean curd cubes to heat through. Taste and adjust with salt if necessary.
4. If using fresh rice noodles, cook in boiling water until noodle is of preferred texture. If using dried noodles, first soak in cold water to soften, then cook in boiling water to preferred texture. Add noodles of your choice or cooked rice to the kimchi soup. Garnish with chopped greens and garlic chunks.
5. Serve immediately.

Mee Goreng Jawa (Javanese-style Fried Wheat Noodles)

Preparation time: 45 minutes   Serves 3–4

This dish can be made with any of the thicker wheat noodles such as the Hokkien *mee*, longevity noodles, udon or dried wheat noodles.

Thick wheat noodles	500 g (1 lb 1¹/₂ oz)
Cooking oil	4 Tbsp
Shallots	2, peeled and thinly sliced
Peeled prawns	100 g (3¹/₂ oz), deveined
Beef	100 g (3¹/₂ oz), thinly sliced
Bean sprouts	100 g (3¹/₂ oz)
Mustard greens	300 g (11 oz), cut into finger lengths

SEASONING

Salt	¹/₂ tsp
Light soy sauce	2 Tbsp
Indonesian dark sweet soy sauce (*kicap manis*)	2 Tbsp
Tomato sauce	2 Tbsp

SPICE PASTE

Shallots	100 g (3¹/₂ oz)
Garlic	4 cloves, peeled
Galangal	4 slices
Dried anchovies (*ikan bilis*)	2 Tbsp
Chilli powder	¹/₂ Tbsp
Water	2 Tbsp

GARNISH AND CONDIMENT

Lime or lemon halves
Red chilli-vinegar sauce (page 15)

1. Make spice paste first. Blend together all ingredients to a smooth paste. Set aside.
2. Prepare seasoning by mixing together ingredients in a small bowl. Set aside.
3. If using dried or semi-dried thick wheat noodles like udon, bring a pot of water to the boil and cook noodles until nearly tender. Drain and stir in 1 Tbsp oil to prevent it from clumping. If using Hokkien *mee*, skip this step.
4. Heat 1 Tbsp oil in a wok and fry shallots until it begins to brown. Stir in noodles and fry for 2 minutes. Dish out and set aside.
5. Heat remaining 2 Tbsp oil in the wok and fry spice paste until fragrant.
6. Stir in prawns and beef and fry until prawns start changing colour. Stir in bean sprouts, mustard greens and seasoning mixture.
7. When mustard greens start to change colour, stir in noodles and mix well.
8. Dish out into a large serving platter or divide into individual servings.
9. Garnish with lime or lemon halves and serve with a condiment such as red chilli-vinegar sauce.

Indian Mee Goreng

Preparation time: 30 minutes   Serves 3–4

The Indian food stalls in Singapore and Malaysia will prepare this dish with a dollop of curry sauce. Substitute with some curry powder if you don't have a convenient pot of curry sitting about. Perhaps this is the origin of those "Singapore noodles" that are found all over the world!

Meat curry powder	2 Tbsp
Salt	$1^1/_2$ tsp
Water	1 Tbsp
Cooking oil	4 Tbsp
Onion	50 g ($1^2/_3$ oz / $^1/_4$ cup), peeled and cubed
Prawns (optional)	200 g (7 oz / 1 cup), peeled, leaving tails on
Peas	100 g ($3^1/_2$ oz / $^1/_2$ cup)
Large tomato	100 g ($3^1/_2$ oz), cubed
Hokkien *mee*	500 g (1 lb $1^1/_2$ oz)
Potato	100 g ($3^1/_2$ oz), boiled, peeled and cubed
Tomato sauce	2 Tbsp
Dark soy sauce	$^1/_2$ tsp
Bean sprouts	300 g (11 oz / $1^1/_2$ cups)
Eggs	2
Green chilli	1, coarsely sliced

GARNISH
Lime halves

1. Mix meat curry powder, salt and water together into a thick paste. Set aside.
2. Heat 3 Tbsp oil in a wok and fry onion until soft. Stir in curry paste and fry until curry is fragrant.
3. Add prawns and when they turn pink, add peas, tomato, noodles, potato, tomato sauce and dark soy sauce. Add bean sprouts last to prevent overcooking.
4. Make a well in the centre of wok, add the last tablespoonful of oil, then break eggs into hot oil, cover with noodles and turn down heat to let eggs set without burning noodles.
5. Stir in green chilli.
6. Serve hot with lime halves on the side.

Tareko Chau Chau (Nepali-style Fried Noodles)

Preparation time: 45 minutes   Serves 3–4

Make these fried noodles with packets of instant noodles (discard the packaged seasoning) or dried wheat noodles. The Nepalis like their noodles in short strands and on the soft side so that it can be eaten with a spoon. You can keep the noodles long and al dente if preferred.

Eggs	3, beaten
Salt	$1^1/_2$ tsp
Ghee/cooking oil	4 Tbsp
Ground cumin	1 tsp
Chilli powder	1 tsp
Water	1 Tbsp
Dried wheat noodles	300 g (11 oz)
Onion	100 g ($3^1/_2$ oz), peeled and thinly sliced
Ginger	4 slices, finely chopped
Cabbage	200 g (7 oz), shredded
Tomato	100 g ($3^1/_2$ oz), cubed
Carrot	100 g ($3^1/_2$ oz), peeled and sliced
Indian garam masala (page 12)	1 tsp

GARNISH

Sliced green chillies
Lemon slices
Onion wedges

1. Before you start boiling the noodles, prepare all the ingredients for cooking.
2. Beat eggs with $^1/_2$ tsp salt. Heat a little ghee/oil in a wok and make several thin omelettes with the beaten eggs. Cut omelettes into thin strips.
3. Mix together ground cumin and chilli powder with 1 tsp salt and 1 Tbsp water. Set aside.
4. Bring a pot of salted water to the boil and add dried noodles. While noodles are returning to the boil, start frying the other ingredients.
5. Heat remaining ghee/oil in the wok and fry onion and ginger until fragrant. Stir in cumin and chilli powder mixture. Mix well.
6. Add vegetables and fry until cabbage is limp but still crisp. Scoop out undercooked noodles and add to the wok with the other ingredients and stir-fry for 1 minute or until noodles are cooked to preferred texture. Sprinkle in a little water if needed.
7. Lastly, stir in egg strips and sprinkle garam masala over fried noodles.
8. Dish out and garnish with sliced green chillies, lemon slices and raw onion wedges.

Kon Loh Meen, Penang-style

(Dry Cantonese Egg Noodles, Penang-style)

Preparation time: 45 minutes   Serves 1

The Penang hawker version of Cantonese dry noodles or *kon loh meen* usually has no chilli sauce in the dressing. Those who want some heat in their noodles must ask for it or eat the noodles with the pickled green chillies that are served as a condiment. Frozen wonton and gyoza can now be found in supermarkets. Use this instead of making your own. This recipe makes a single serving. Repeat to prepare more servings as necessary.

Mustard greens	100 g (3^1/$_2$ oz), cut into finger-lengths
Thin Cantonese fresh egg noodles (*mee kia*)	120 g (4^1/$_3$ oz)
Chinese-style red roast pork (page 22)	50 g (1^2/$_3$ oz), thinly sliced
Chinese-style chicken vegetable soup (page 23)	1 small bowl
Pickled green chillies (page 25)	

DRESSING

Lard	1^1/$_2$ Tbsp
Sesame oil	1 tsp
Dark soy sauce	^{1}/$_2$ Tbsp
Light soy sauce	1 Tbsp
Ground white pepper	^{1}/$_2$ tsp

1. Mix together dressing ingredients in a bowl or soup plate.
2. Bring a large pot of water to the boil. Blanch mustard greens for 10 seconds. Scoop out and set aside.
3. Return water to the boil and blanch noodles until tender but al dente. This takes about 1 minute depending on the thickness of the noodles.
4. Scoop out noodles and rinse under cold water or drop noodles into a cold water bath. Scoop out and pop noodles back into boiling water for a few seconds.
5. Remove and drain the noodles well. Stir the noodles into the dressing.
6. Garnish with blanched mustard greens and roast pork.
7. Serve with a small bowl of soup and pickled green chillies in light soy sauce on the side.

Longevity Noodles

Preparation time: 45 minutes   Serves 3–4

These very long semi-dried coarse wheat noodles known as longevity noodles used to appear around the Chinese New Year season when it was a tradition in the Hokkien community to eat them at least once during the 15-day Chinese New Year celebrations. They are also popular for birthday celebrations. These noodles which come folded up must be cut before you start boiling them. Otherwise, the noodles are too long and unwieldy to fry. Cut them at one end of the folds.

Thick wheat noodles (*mee sua*)	500 g (1 lb 1¹/₂ oz)
Cooking oil	5 Tbsp
Chopped garlic	1 Tbsp
Pork	100 g (3¹/₂ oz), thinly sliced
Dried shiitake mushrooms	4, softened in cold water and sliced
Peeled prawns	200 g (7 oz), deveined
Mustard greens	200 g (7 oz), cut into finger lengths
Carrot	100 g (3¹/₂ oz), peeled and sliced
Salt	1 tsp
Light soy sauce	2 Tbsp
Dark soy sauce	a few drops

CONDIMENTS (OPTIONAL)

Sambal belacan with lime juice
   (page 13)

Pickled green chillies (page 25)

Red chillies with fish sauce
   (page 15)

Red chilli-vinegar sauce
   (page 15)

Vinegar-chilli dip (page 16)

Kimchi

1. Prepare other ingredients for frying before starting to boil noodles.
2. Bring a pot of salted water to the boil and put noodles in to boil. Start frying other ingredients as soon as you put the noodles into the pot.
3. Heat oil in a wok and sauté garlic until fragrant. Add pork and mushrooms and sauté until pork changes colour.
4. Add prawns and when prawns change colour, stir in vegetables and salt and mix well.
5. Scoop the slightly undercooked noodles from the pot and place into wok. Add soy sauces and mix well. Continue frying until noodles are tender or about 2–3 minutes.
6. Serve hot with a condiment of your choice.

Pancit Guisado (Fried Noodles, Filipino-style)

Preparation time: 30 minutes   Serves 3–4

Pancit means noodles and *guisado* means fried. The noodles used can be thin rice vermicelli, egg noodles, wheat noodles (*mee sua*) or glass noodles. The word *guisado* and the addition of bay leaves are clues to the Spanish colonial heritage of the Philippines. No other South East Asian country uses bay leaves in its ethnic cuisine.

Dried shiitake mushrooms	2
Water	375 ml (12 fl oz / 1$\frac{1}{2}$ cups)
Pork	100 g (3$\frac{1}{2}$ oz)
Chicken	100 g (3$\frac{1}{2}$ oz)
Cooking oil	2 Tbsp
Large onion	100 g (3$\frac{1}{2}$ oz), peeled and finely chopped
Chopped garlic	2 Tbsp
Chinese dried sausage	2, thinly sliced
Bay leaves	2, crushed
Snow peas	$\frac{1}{2}$ cup
Cabbage	100 g (3$\frac{1}{2}$ oz), shredded
Carrot	50 g (1$\frac{2}{3}$ oz), peeled and julienned
Dried thin/medium rice vermicelli	300 g (11 oz), softened in cold water until pliable
Salt	1$\frac{1}{2}$ tsp
Ground white pepper	1 tsp
Sesame oil	1 tsp
Red chillies with soy sauce (page 15)	

GARNISH

Spring onion	1, chopped
Coriander leaves	1 bunch, chopped
Eggs	2, hard-boiled, peeled and sliced
Lime halves	

1. Rinse mushrooms and soften in 125 ml (4 fl oz / $\frac{1}{2}$ cup) water. Slice softened mushrooms and reserve soaking water for the gravy.

2. Bring 250 ml (8 fl oz / 1 cup) water to the boil and boil pork and chicken until cooked. Cool and cut pork into thin, narrow strips and chicken into cubes. Reserve broth for the gravy.

3. Heat oil in a wok and fry onion and garlic until onion begins to turn transparent and garlic is browning. Stir in Chinese sausage, fry for a minute, then add bay leaves, reserved broth and mushroom water and bring to the boil.

4. Add mushrooms, snow peas, cabbage, and carrot and cook for 1 minute.

5. Stir in rice vermicelli, salt and pepper and fry until noodles are tender but still al dente. Stir in cooked pork and chicken and sesame oil and mix well.

6. Dish out onto a large serving platter and top with garnishes. Serve with a condiment of red chillies with soy sauce.

Fried Udon with Kimchi and Mushrooms, Korean-style

Preparation time: 45 minutes   Serves 3–4

Vary the vegetables with what you have in the fridge but keep in mind colour combinations as well as blending flavours. If you substitute udon with soba, you get *yaki* soba. For dashi use Japanese bottled soup concentrate which is available from Japanese supermarkets to speed things up.

Kimchi	300 g (11 oz)
Pork/prawns	300 g (11 oz)
Sesame oil	1 tsp
Cooked dried red chilli paste (page 14)	2 tsp
Salt	3/4 tsp
Dried udon	300 g (11 oz)
Cooking oil	3 Tbsp
Onion	30 g (1 oz), peeled and thinly sliced
Dried shiitake mushrooms	4, softened in water and thickly sliced
Light soy sauce	1 1/2 Tbsp
Garlic	3 cloves, peeled and cut into slivers
Spring onion	1, small, cut into finger lengths
Coriander leaves	1 small bunch, cut into finger lengths
Korean sesame salt (page 17)	

1. If the kimchi is too chunky, cut into thinner slices. Squeeze out the juices but keep for use later, if needed.
2. If using pork, cut into julienne strips. If using prawns, peel but keep the tails on. Mix sesame oil, chilli paste and 1/4 tsp salt into pork/prawns. Marinate for 15 minutes.
3. Bring a pot of water to the boil and boil udon until tender but al dente.
4. While udon is boiling, heat oil in a wok and sauté onion for 1 minute, then add pork/prawns and mushrooms and stir-fry until meat is cooked.
5. Add kimchi, drained udon, soy sauce and remaining salt and mix well. Stir-fry for 2 minutes or until kimchi is thoroughly heated.
6. Stir in garlic, spring onion and coriander leaves.
7. Dish out and serve with Korean sesame salt.

Thai-style Rice Noodles in Soup

Preparation time: 45 minutes　　　　　Serves 3–4

What makes this a Thai-style noodle soup is the seasoning that includes sugar and fish sauce as well as the condiment of fish sauce, vinegar and bird's eye chillies. Any kind of rice noodles — mouse-tail, rice vermicelli, broad rice noodles (*kuay tiao*) will taste good in this soup. It is quick to prepare if you buy ready-cooked red roast pork and have ground roasted peanuts in the fridge. Note that while the soup serves between 3 and 4, the dressing for the noodles is per serving. Repeat as needed.

Bean sprouts	200 g (7 oz), rinsed
Any kind of fresh rice noodles	500 g (1 lb 1½ oz)
Chinese-style red roast pork (page 22)	200 g (7 oz), sliced
Lettuce leaves	a small bunch, shredded
Spring onion	1, chopped
Coriander leaves	1 bunch, chopped
Fried garlic (page 11)	½ Tbsp
Ground toasted peanuts (page 10)	3 Tbsp

SOUP

Chicken stock (page 20)	1 litre (32 fl oz / 4 cups)
Salt	1½ tsp
Sugar	3 tsp
White rice vinegar	1 tsp

DRESSING (SERVES 1)

Toasted red chilli flakes (page 17)	1 tsp
Fish sauce	1 Tbsp
Garlic oil (page 11)	1 Tbsp

CONDIMENTS (OPTIONAL)

Vinegar-chilli dip (page 16)
Red chillies with fish sauce (page 15)
Red chilli-vinegar sauce (page 15)
Toasted red chilli flakes (page 17)

1. Prepare soup. Bring stock to the boil in a pot, then stir in salt, sugar and vinegar. Lower heat and leave stock to simmer.

2. Prepare dressing. Put dressing ingredients into a serving bowl. Repeat for the number of servings.

3. Bring a large pot of water to the boil. Blanch bean sprouts for 10 seconds, then drain well and divide into serving bowls. Return water to the boil and blanch noodles until tender but al dente. Drain well and divide into serving bowls.

4. Ladle hot soup over noodles and garnish with roast pork, lettuce, spring onion, coriander leaves, fried garlic and ground peanuts.

5. Serve immediately with a condiment of your choice.

Soup Noodles, Javanese-style

Preparation time: 45 minutes   Serves 3–4

This is essentially a vegetable soup with noodles added to it. It can be any kind of noodles, fresh or dried. If noodles are dried, soften in cold water. This basic soup can also be used to make a rice soup by substituting noodles with some cooked rice.

Prawn/chicken stock (page 20)	1 litre (32 fl oz / 4 cups)
Fried shallots (page 11)	2 Tbsp
Tomato	100 g (3$^1/_2$ oz), chopped
Red chillies	2, seeded and sliced
Potato	50 g (1$^2/_3$ oz), peeled and cubed
Salt	1$^1/_2$ tsp
Ground black pepper	2 tsp
Peeled prawns	200 g (7 oz), deveined
Bean sprouts	50 g (1$^2/_3$ oz), rinsed
Mustard greens	50 g (1$^2/_3$ oz), cut into finger lengths
Cabbage	50 g (1$^2/_3$ oz), shredded
Any kind of fresh noodles	500 g (1 lb 1$^1/_2$ oz) or 300 g (11 oz) dried noodles, softened in cold water
Firm bean curd	50 g (1$^2/_3$ oz), cubed

GARNISH

Tomato	1, quartered or sliced
Eggs	2, hard-boiled, peeled and sliced
Spring onion	1, chopped

1. Put stock, fried shallots, tomato, chillies, potato, salt and pepper into a saucepan and simmer for 15 minutes or until potato cubes are beginning to get tender.
2. Add prawns and when they turn pink, stir in bean sprouts, mustard greens and cabbage and bring to the boil.
3. Add noodles and bean curd and return to the boil. Simmer until noodles are tender but still all dente.
4. Divide into serving bowls and serve immediately.
5. Garnish with tomato, eggs and a sprinkling of chopped spring onion.

Tau Pok Soup with Noodles or Rice

Preparation time: 30 minutes   Serves 3–4

This soup can be served by itself as a one-dish meal or with noodles or rice added. Deep-fried soy bean puffs (*tau pok* in Hokkien or *inari* in Japanese) stuffed with fish paste are part of an array of fish-paste stuffed items called *yong tau foo* in Singapore and Malaysia. All *yong tau foo* ingredients make good soup but stuffed *tau pok* is the most convenient because they freeze well. Stuffed soy bean puffs come in small squares or large triangles which are cut from larger square puffs.

Cooking oil	1 Tbsp
Chopped garlic	1 Tbsp
Chicken stock (page 20)	1 litre (32 fl oz / 4 cups)
Salt	1$\frac{1}{2}$ tsp
Stuffed deep-fried soy bean puffs	16 triangles
Mustard greens	200 g (7 oz), cut into finger lengths
Spring onion	1, chopped
Coriander leaves	1 bunch, chopped
Red chillies with soy sauce (page 15)	

NOODLES OR RICE

Fresh rice noodles	500 g (1 lb 1$\frac{1}{2}$ oz), blanched
Dried wheat or rice noodles	300 g (11 oz), boiled
Cooked rice	3 cups (from 225 g / 8 oz / 1$\frac{1}{2}$ rice cooker cups rice)

1. In a saucepan, heat oil and sauté garlic until it begins to brown. Add chicken stock and salt and bring to the boil.
2. Add soy bean puffs and simmer until fish paste is cooked.
3. Add mustard greens, spring onion and coriander leaves and bring to the boil. Turn off heat.
4. Dish cooked noodles or rice into serving bowls and top with hot soup, soy bean puffs and vegetables.
5. Serve with a condiment of red chillies with soy sauce.

Fried Broad Rice Noodles with Chives and Salted Fish

Preparation time: 45 minutes   Serves 3–4

Mustard cabbage is often sold as just stems partly because the leaves shorten shelf life. It is a bitter vegetable so if you do not like bitter vegetables, substitute with Tientsin cabbage (bok choy) or broccoli.

Salted fish	100 g (3^1/$_2$ oz)
Cooking oil	4 Tbsp
Mustard cabbage stems	200 g (7 oz), thinly sliced
Carrot	50 g (1^2/$_3$ oz), peeled and sliced
Chopped garlic	2 Tbsp
Boneless firm-fleshed white fish or fish cake	200 g (7 oz), sliced
Fresh broad rice noodles	500 g (1 lb 1^1/$_2$ oz)
Salt	1 tsp
Ground white pepper	^{1}/$_2$ tsp
Chives	100 g (3^1/$_2$ oz), cut into finger lengths

CONDIMENTS (OPTIONAL)
Red chillies with soy sauce
(page 15)
Vinegar-chilli dip (page 16)
Pickled green chillies (page 25)

1. Rinse salted fish well and pat dry. Pull out bones if any. Slice thinly.
2. Heat oil in a wok and deep-fry salted fish until brown and fragrant. Take out, cool, then pound salted fish or shred by hand. Set aside.
3. Bring a pot of salted water to the boil, then blanch mustard cabbage stems and carrot for 10 seconds. Scoop out and set aside.
4. In the wok with the oil used to fry the salted fish, sauté chopped garlic until it begins to brown. Add blanched vegetables and stir-fry for 1 minute. Dish out and set aside.
5. Fry fish or fish cake in the remaining oil for about 1 minute. Add noodles, salt and pepper and mix well. Stir in vegetables, chives and salted fish. Mix well. When chives begin to turn limp, turn off heat.
6. Dish out into a large serving platter and set out individual serving plates.
7. Serve with a condiment of your choice.

Spicy Sichuan Vegetable Soup with Rice or Noodles

Preparation time: 30 minutes   Serves 3–4

Add cooked rice, long or short-grain, or noodles to this soup to complete the dish. Preserved Sichuan vegetable is pickled in salt and chilli powder and should be soaked in several changes of cold water to get rid of excess salt. On the other hand, do not over-soak until it turns bland. It's the right amount of salt that makes this crunchy vegetable tasty. Do the taste test during the soaking.

Preserved Sichuan vegetable	100 g (3^1/$_2$ oz)
Pork/chicken stock (pages 20–21)	1.25 litres (40 fl oz / 5 cups)
Soft bean curd	200 g (7 oz), cubed
Chrysanthemum leaves	100 g (3^1/$_2$ oz)

NOODLES OR RICE
Fresh rice noodles	500 g (1 lb 1^1/$_2$ oz), blanched
Dried wheat or rice noodles	300 g (11 oz), boiled
Cooked rice (long or short-grain)	2 cups (from 150 g / 5^1/$_3$ oz / 1 rice cooker cup rice)

MEAT AND MARINADE
Pork/chicken	150 g (5^1/$_3$ oz), cut into matchsticks
Light soy sauce	1 tsp
Dark soy sauce	a few drops
Cornflour	1 tsp
Sesame oil	2 tsp
Salt	a pinch

GARNISH AND CONDIMENT
Fried garlic (page 11)
Chopped coriander leaves
Chopped spring onions
Red chillies with soy sauce
  (page 15)

1. Mix meat and marinade ingredients together and stand for 10 minutes.
2. Prepare soup before blanching noodles. Rinse Sichuan vegetable clean and slice thinly. Soak in several changes of water to leach out some of the salt. Do not over-soak. Bring stock to the boil, add Sichuan vegetable and simmer for 5 minutes before stirring in marinated meat and bean curd. Bring to the boil and simmer for 1 minute before adding chrysanthemum leaves. Turn off heat when leaves change colour or in about 10 seconds.
3. To blanch noodles, bring a pot of water to the boil. Put noodles into the boiling water and cook for 1–2 minutes depending on the type of noodles.
4. Ladle hot soup over boiled noodles or cooked rice and garnish with fried garlic, chopped spring onions and coriander leaves. Serve with a condiment of red chillies with soy sauce.

Penang Birthday Mee Sua (Penang-style Birthday Noodle Soup)

Preparation time: 30 minutes   Serves 1

Although this is the traditional noodle soup served to the birthday person among the Penang Straits Chinese, it makes a tasty meal for any other day. For a less elaborate dish, drop ingredients like kidney or even liver and just go with the minced pork and egg. Instead of hard-boiling the egg, just crack the raw egg into the boiling soup before you add the noodles. This recipe makes a single serving. Note that fine wheat vermicelli cooks very quickly and it does not sit well.

Pig's kidney	1
Cooking oil	$\frac{1}{2}$ Tbsp
Chopped garlic	2 tsp
Ginger	2 slices
Pork stock (page 21)	500 ml (16 fl oz / 2 cups)
Minced pork	1 Tbsp
Pig's liver	30 g (1 oz), sliced
Salt	$\frac{1}{2}$ tsp
Ground white pepper	$\frac{1}{4}$ tsp
Fine wheat vermicelli (*mee sua*)	50 g (1$\frac{2}{3}$ oz)
Chopped spring onion	
Egg	1, hard-boiled and dyed red with food colour
Dark soy sauce	as needed

1. To clean kidney, split it in half crosswise to trim off smelly renal tubes. Cut away white parts. Using a sharp knife, score kidney in a criss-cross pattern and cut into bite-size rectangles. Soak pieces of kidney in several changes of cold water until kidney is free of any strong smell.

2. Heat oil in a small pot and fry garlic and ginger until light brown. Pour in stock and bring to the boil. Drop in minced pork and stir quickly to break it up in the soup.

3. Add kidney, liver, salt and pepper and cook for 1 minute.

4. Remove red thread from around bundles of noodles and rinse quickly under a cold tap. Drop noodles into boiling soup. Stir and cook for 1 minute.

5. Dish out and garnish with spring onion. The egg can be shelled and served in the soup or unshelled and served on the side. Serve immediately with dark soy sauce for the dip.

Pyongyang Nyaeng Myon

(Cold Buckwheat Noodles, Pyongyang-style)

Preparation time: 3 hours   Serves 3–4

This is a perfect dish for a box of beef stock that you may have stashed in the freezer. Defrost, remove the layer of fat on top and filter the stock through a coffee filter or a piece of muslin held over an appropriately-sized sieve. Replace the beef brisket with a piece of lightly blanched beef for garnishing the dish if using frozen stock. Or you can make it from scratch. Using a slow cooker will reduce the need to keep an eye on the boiling. Substitute Korean pear with other Asian pears if unavailable.

Dried buckwheat noodles	300 g (11 oz)
Korean pear	8 thin slices
Pickled radish (page 25)	
Soft bean curd	150 g (5^1/$_3$ oz), cubed
Spring onion	1, chopped
Korean sesame salt (page 17) or *shichimi togarashi* (page 16)	

BROTH

Beef bones	500 g (1 lb 1^1/$_2$ oz)
Beef brisket	500 g (1 lb 1^1/$_2$ oz)
Water	2 litres (64 fl oz / 8 cups)
Old ginger	4 slices
Garlic	3 cloves, peeled
Whole black peppercorns	^{1}/$_2$ tsp
White rice vinegar	1^1/$_2$ Tbsp
Light soy sauce	1–1^1/$_2$ Tbsp
Salt	^{1}/$_2$ tsp

1. Put all broth ingredients into a stockpot and bring to the boil. Turn down heat and simmer gently for about 3 hours or until stock is reduced to half and beef brisket is tender. Remove beef brisket and discard bones. Cool and refrigerate overnight.

2. The next day, scoop out the congealed fat, then strain broth through a piece of muslin or paper coffee filter. Slice beef brisket thinly.

3. Prepare noodles. Have ready an ice-cold water bath. Bring a large pot of water to the boil and boil noodles until done but still al dente. Scoop out and drop into the ice-water bath. Drain well and divide into serving bowls, twirling noodles into a heap.

4. Ladle ice-cold broth into the bowl but do not cover the top of the heap of noodles. Place slices of pear, beef brisket and a few strands of pickled radish on the top of the noodles. Float cubes of bean curd in broth. Sprinkle in chopped spring onion.

5. Serve cold with Korean sesame salt or *shichimi togarashi*.

West Asian Rice Salad

Preparation time: 30 minutes   Serves 4–5

This rice salad is nothing like Malay or Straits Chinese rice salad (also called *nasi ulam*) in flavour. Make it a complete vegetarian meal with the addition of boiled beans such as chickpeas or lentils or with a few boiled prawns or leftover grilled meat. Tomatoes and cucumber can be substituted with other vegetables such as capsicums and blanched beans or peas. Omit sumac if not available. Sumac gives the rice salad a lovely red glow as well as a delicate tang.

Warm cooked long-grain rice	4 cups (from 300 g / 11 oz / 2 rice cooker cups rice)
Tomatoes	100 g (3^1/$_2$ oz), seeded and chopped
Cucumber	100 g (3^1/$_2$ oz), chopped
Pickled lemon (optional)	1 slice, chopped or ^{1}/$_4$ cup pickled green beans (page 25), chopped
Onion	100 g (3^1/$_2$ oz), peeled and chopped
Red chilli	1, seeded and chopped
Boiled beans/grilled chicken (page 23)/grilled meat/ boiled prawns (page 20) (optional)	2 cups
Sumac	1^1/$_2$ Tbsp
Mint	^{1}/$_2$ cup, chopped
Parsley/coriander leaves	^{1}/$_2$ cup, chopped
Black olives	^{1}/$_4$ cup, pitted and sliced thinly
Cooked yoghurt sauce (page 19) or cucumber raita (page 18) (optional)	

DRESSING

Olive oil	2 Tbsp
Lemon juice	1^1/$_2$ Tbsp
Chilli powder	^{1}/$_4$ tsp
Ground cumin	1 tsp
Salt	1^1/$_2$ tsp

1. Mix together dressing in a small jar and shake well.
2. In a large mixing bowl, stir half the dressing into warm rice. Add tomatoes, cucumber, pickled lemon or green beans, onion and chilli, boiled beans or meat if using, and the rest of the dressing. Stir in sumac and herbs last.
3. Arrange rice salad on a serving plate and garnish with black olives.
4. If available, serve rice salad with cooked yoghurt sauce or cucumber raita.

Black Rice Salad

Preparation time: 1–2 hours   Serves 3–4

The most time-consuming part about this recipes is getting the black rice to soften. If you have a slow cooker or a rice pot with a brown rice setting, it will be on autopilot. Reduce the water added if cooking brown rice. The nutty texture of black and brown rice and the fact that the salad tastes better if left to sit for a while makes it good picnic food. It makes great leftovers too.

Black/brown rice	300 g (11 oz) or 2 rice cooker cups, soaked overnight or at least for 1 hour
Water	1 litre (32 fl oz / 4 cups)
Onion	50 g (1²/₃ oz), peeled and thinly sliced
Cucumber	200 g (7 oz), cored and cubed
Red/yellow capsicum	1, seeded and cubed
Carrots	200 g (7 oz), peeled and cubed or sliced
Black olives	¹/₂ cup, seeded and sliced
Parsley/coriander leaves	¹/₂ cup, chopped

DRESSING

Olive oil	3 Tbsp
Lemon juice	2 Tbsp
Salt	1¹/₂ tsp
Chilli powder	1 tsp

1. Cook rice with water using your preferred method. When rice is done, fluff it up and let it rest for 10 minutes.
2. Mix the dressing ingredients together in a mixing bowl. Adjust seasoning to taste. Stir in onion and half the dressing into the warm rice and mix well before adding vegetables and herbs.
3. Rest salad for at least an hour in the refrigerator to let the flavours mature.
4. Serve cold.

Stuffed Tau Pok (Singapore-style Stuffed Fried Bean Curd)

Preparation time: 45 minutes   Serves 3–4

This delicious salad is easily made at home and makes a good one-dish meal. Get the larger square flat *tau pok*, not the smaller cubes. To up the vegetable content, increase the amount of bean sprouts and cucumber and turn what can't be stuffed into the bean curd squares into a salad by mixing with some of the prawn paste dressing.

Cucumber	300 g (11 oz), shredded
Bean sprouts	300 g (11 oz), blanched
Lettuce leaves	3, coarsely shredded
Deep-fried spongy bean curd	12 pieces, slit on one side

DRESSING

Tamarind juice (page 10)	4 Tbsp
Lime juice	3 Tbsp
Black prawn paste (*haeko*)	4 Tbsp
Sugar	2 Tbsp
Sambal belacan (page 13)	1$\frac{1}{2}$ Tbsp
Toasted peanuts (page 10)	250 g (9 oz), finely ground

1. Mix shredded cucumber with cooled blanched bean sprouts and shredded lettuce.
2. Slit one side of deep-fried bean curd with the tip of a sharp knife and stuff with mixed vegetables. Set aside until it is time to grill them.
3. Prepare dressing. Stir tamarind juice and lime juice into black prawn paste to thin it out. Add sugar, *sambal belacan* and lastly, peanuts. Adjust seasoning to taste.
4. Grill stuffed deep-fried bean curd in an oven-toaster or under a grill to crisp them.
5. Pour dressing over deep-fried bean curd and serve immediately.

Burmese Bean Curd Salad

Preparation time: 45 minutes   Serves 3–4

This unusual salad combines bean curd treated in two different ways — raw and deep-fried, tender and chewy, plus the crunch of the lightly salted cucumber shreds. The kind of cooked oil used for the dressing will affect the final flavour of the salad. So if you use garlic oil, it won't taste the same as if you had used shallot oil or oil in which you had fried some meat.

Bean curd	400 g (14$^1/_3$ oz)
Cooking oil for frying	
Salt	$^1/_2$ tsp
Cucumber	300 g (11 oz), coarsely shredded
Cooked oil dressing (page 14)	3 Tbsp
Shallots	3, peeled and thinly sliced
Red bird's eye chilli	1, seeded and chopped
Coriander leaves	1 bunch, chopped
Spring onion	1, chopped
Toasted grated coconut/ toasted ground peanuts (page 10) (optional)	to taste
Fried garlic (page 11)	1 Tbsp

1. Divide bean curd in two lots. Cube one half into bite-size pieces and set aside.

2. Heat oil in a wok and deep-fry other half of the bean curd. Cool, then cut into cubes or thin strips.

3. Stir salt into shredded cucumber. Stand for 10 minutes, then squeeze out the water.

4. In a mixing bowl, combine cucumber and both lots of bean curd. Toss with cooked oil dressing, taking care not to mash uncooked bean curd too much. Add shallots, chilli, coriander leaves and spring onion and mix well.

5. If adding coconut or peanuts, add now and mix well. Top with fried garlic.

TIP

To make a bean curd and bean sprout salad, substitute the cucumber with 300 g (11 oz) bean sprouts. Blanch the bean sprouts for 10 seconds in a pot of boiling water and drain well.

Cambodian Chicken and Pineapple Salad

Preparation time: 30 minutes   Serves 3–4

This salad is good on its own as a one-dish meal or served with rice. The carrots and pineapple combination can also be substituted with other combinations such as green mango with cucumber or cabbage, or broccoli with pineapple. Only green mango shreds need to be pounded, like carrot shreds.

Carrots	300 g (11 oz), peeled and shredded
Cooked oil dressing (page 14) or Indo-Chinese Dressing (page 15)	3 Tbsp
Ripe/canned pineapple	200 g (7 oz), shredded
Shallots	50 g ($1^2/_3$ oz), peeled and thinly sliced
Grilled chicken	300 g (11 oz), shredded or thinly sliced
Mint	$^1/_2$ cup
Basil	$^1/_2$ cup
Toasted and ground peanuts (page 10), or toasted grated coconut (page 10), ground fine	4 Tbsp

1. In a Thai-style mortar, pound shredded carrots with half the dressing until soft.
2. Stir in pineapple, shallots, chicken, mint and basil. Add remaining dressing.
3. Dish out and sprinkle peanuts into salad before serving.

Burmese Potato Salad

Preparation time: 30 minutes   Serves 3–4

Like most Asians, the Burmese think of potatoes as a vegetable to be eaten with rice. This potato salad makes a good dish on its own if you add some grilled or boiled meat to it.

Cooked oil dressing (page 14)	4 Tbsp
Potatoes	500 g (1 lb 1$\frac{1}{2}$ oz), boiled and cubed
Green chillies	2, seeded and chopped
Onion	50 g (1$\frac{2}{3}$ oz / $\frac{1}{4}$ cup), chopped
Fried shallots (page 11)	1 Tbsp
Mint	$\frac{1}{2}$ cup, chopped
Grilled meat/chicken (page 23) (optional)	

1. Dress peeled and cubed potatoes while they are still warm.
2. Stir in chillies, onion, fried shallots, mint and thin slices of grilled meat/chicken if using.

Vietnamese Kangkong and Beef Salad

Preparation time: 45 minutes   Serves 3–4

In the Indo-Chinese countries, there are several kinds of water convolvulus, one of which comes with very few leaves. Use this kind for this salad if it is available. If not, the leafy kind familiar in Singapore is also tasty with the leaves raw. Whichever kind is used, the stems have to be split thinly and curled in cold water. This salad makes a good low carbohydrate meal.

Beef	300 g (11 oz), cut into thin strips
Sugar	1 Tbsp
Fish sauce	1/2 Tbsp
Chopped garlic	1 tsp
Cooking oil	1 Tbsp
Water convolvulus stems	500 g (1 lb 1 1/2 oz)
Tomato	1, seeded and cut into thin wedges
Onion	50 g (1 2/3 oz), peeled and thinly sliced
Indo-Chinese dressing (page 15)	4 Tbsp
Coriander leaves	1 small bunch, chopped
Fried shallots (page 11)	2 Tbsp
Toasted and ground peanuts (page 10)	3 Tbsp

1. Prepare dressing. Mix dressing ingredients in a bottle with a lid and shake. Refrigerate until needed.

2. Season beef with sugar, fish sauce and garlic for 30 minutes.

3. Heat oil in a frying pan and sauté seasoned beef for 2 or more minutes, depending on how well done you like your beef. Set aside to cool.

4. Rinse water convolvulus clean and discard any discoloured or rotten leaves. If using leafy variety, pluck leaves from stem and rinse clean again. Split stems into quarters lengthwise and cut into 12-cm (5-in) lengths. Soak stems in cold water to curl them. Drain well and spin leaves and stems in a salad spinner to get rid of the water.

5. In a mixing bowl, toss tomato, onion and water convolvulus with Indo-Chinese dressing. Add cooked beef, coriander leaves, fried shallots and peanuts.

6. Dish out and serve.

Penang Fruit Rojak

Preparation time: 1 hour   Serves 3–4

This makes a great one-dish meal whether as a snack or the entrée. Penang *rojak* requires only a mix of fruit. Substitute suggested fruit with other firm and preferably tart fruit such as green apples or unripe pears. The Singapore version is more time-consuming to prepare as it calls for blanched vegetables, raw fruit and vegetables and even fried crullers and fried bean curd.

ANY COMBINATION OF THE FOLLOWING TO ADD UP TO 1 KG (2 LB 3 OZ)
Green mango
Buah kedondong
Pineapple
Starfruit
Jambu ayer
Guava

DRESSING

Sugar	3 Tbsp
Tamarind juice (page 10)	$1/_2$ Tbsp
Black prawn paste	75 g ($2^2/_3$ oz/ $1/_3$ cup)
Cooked dried red chilli paste (page 14)	1 Tbsp
Lime juice	2 Tbsp
Chopped torch ginger bud	1 Tbsp
Toasted and ground peanuts	250 g (9 oz / $1^1/_4$ cups)

1. Peel mango, *buah kedondong* and pineapple and cut into bite-size pieces. Starfruit, *jambu ayer* and guava do not require peeling.

2. In a large mixing bowl, mix together dressing starting with sugar, tamarind juice and black prawn paste and ending with the peanuts. Adjust the amount of lime juice according to the amount of sour fruit. If the black prawn paste is very salty, reduce the amount added or thin it out with some water and increase the amount of peanuts.

3. Stir the cut fruit into the dressing and mix well.

4. Dish out and serve.

Tabouleh (Lebanese-Syrian Parsley, Mint and Burghul Salad)

Preparation time: 30 minutes   Serves 3–4

Tabouleh is served in West Asia as an appetiser and eaten scooped up in a lettuce leaf or stuffed into pita bread when it becomes a sandwich filling. Grilled meat and yoghurt sauce can also be added to the filling. The amount of lemon juice here gives quite a sharp salad which is good with meat. Reduce the lemon juice to taste.

Fine burghul	50 g (1²/₃ oz / ¹/₄ cup)
Onion/spring onion	125 g (4¹/₂ oz) peeled, if onion, finely chopped
Parsley	50 g (1²/₃ oz / ¹/₄ cup), chopped
Mint	50 g (1²/₃ oz / ¹/₄ cup), chopped
Tomatoes	100 g (3¹/₂ oz / ¹/₂ cup), seeded and chopped
Romaine lettuce	200 g (7 oz)
Pita bread	

DRESSING

Lemon juice	85 ml (2¹/₂ fl oz / ¹/₃ cup)
Olive oil	4 Tbsp
Salt	1 tsp
Ground black pepper	¹/₄ tsp

1. Stir together ingredients for dressing.
2. Measure out burghul into a bowl and stir in 3 Tbsp dressing. Stand for at least 30 minutes or until burghul softens and swells up.
3. When burghul is tender, stir in chopped onion/spring onion, mint, parsley and tomatoes.
4. To use tabouleh as a pita bread filling, shred lettuce coarsely and stir into the rest of the salad.

Fatoush / Lebanese-Syrian Bread Salad

Preparation time: 30 minutes   Serves 3–4

This West Asian salad can be varied with a mix of crisp vegetables and salad leaves but there should be at least one or two herbs like mint and parsley. The bread can also be softened in dressing or kept crunchy. It is a good way to use up leftover pita bread.

Tomatoes	150 g (5 oz), seeded and chopped coarsely
Cucumber	100 g (3$^1/_2$ oz), cored and chopped coarsely
Red capsicum	1, seeded and chopped coarsely
Romaine lettuce	4 large leaves, shredded
Spring onion	1, small, chopped
Parsley	$^1/_2$ cup, chopped
Mint	$^1/_2$ cup, chopped
Coriander leaves	$^1/_2$ cup, chopped
Pita bread	2 pieces, split and toasted
Grilled meat/chicken (page 23)	to taste, shredded or thinly sliced

DRESSING

Olive oil	2 Tbsp
Lemon juice	1 Tbsp
Salt	$^1/_2$ tsp
Ground cumin	$^1/_4$ tsp

CONDIMENTS

Garlic yoghurt dressing
  (page 18)
Garlic/onion yoghurt dip
  (page 19)

1. Mix dressing by shaking together in a bottle.
2. In a mixing bowl, stir together prepared vegetables and herbs with 2 Tbsp dressing. Dish out into a serving bowl.
3. Crush toasted pita bread into large pieces and sprinkle them on the salad. Drizzle the last spoonful of dressing over the bread.
4. Fatoush can be served by itself or packed into another piece of pita bread to make a sandwich. Add some grilled meat/chicken or a couple of balls of falafel if available.
5. If made into a sandwich, serve with a yoghurt dressing or dip.

Mujadara (West Asian Lentil Porridge)

Preparation time: 1 hour   Serves 3–4

Turn this into a porridge or pilaf depending on your preference. If making it as a pilaf, pre-soak or pre-cook the lentils so that the lentils will soften at the same rate as the rice. If made into porridge as in this recipe, boil the rice and lentils together until, like five-grain rice, the harder ingredient is tender. This porridge can also be made with leftover rice.

Brown lentils	100 g (3½ oz / ½ cup), soaked in cold water for 1 hour
Water	1 litre (32 fl oz / 4 cups)
Long-grain rice	200 g (7 oz / 1 cup / 1⅓ rice cooker cups)
Olive oil	2 Tbsp
Onion	30 g (1 oz), peeled and chopped
Garlic	2 cloves, peeled and chopped
Tomatoes	100 g (3½ oz), chopped
Ground turmeric	a pinch
Salt	1 tsp
Ground cumin	¼ tsp
Pickled vegetables (page 25) or grilled chicken/meat (page 23) (optional)	

GARNISH
Chopped parsley/mint/
  coriander leaves

1. Boil lentils in the water and skim off any scum that rises to the top. When water is scum-free, add rice and bring to the boil. Turn down heat and simmer until rice and lentils are soft.

2. Heat olive oil in a frying pan and fry onion and garlic until fragrant. Add tomatoes, turmeric, salt and cumin and cook until tomatoes begin to get mushy. Pour contents of pan into porridge and continue boiling porridge for another 5 minutes.

3. Garnish with chopped herbs and serve porridge hot with pickled vegetables or grilled chicken/meat.

Korean Prawn Porridge

Preparation time: 30 minutes   Serves 3–4

This porridge is quick and tasty. It is deficient in fibre but if you have some kimchi as a condiment, it becomes a complete meal. Stretch the prawns by chopping them up coarsely, if desired. Porridge can also be made with leftover cooked short-grain rice.

Short-grain rice	250 g (9 oz / 1¼ cups)
Water	750 ml (24 fl oz / 3 cups)
Sesame oil	1 Tbsp
Ginger	6 slices, finely shredded
Garlic	1 clove, peeled and finely chopped
Peeled prawns	300 g (11 oz), deveined
Salt	1 tsp
Light soy sauce	1 Tbsp
Pickled vegetables (page 25) or kimchi (optional)	

GARNISH
Chopped spring onions
Korean sesame salt (page 17)

1. Combine rice and water and cook rice porridge using your preferred method to get a smooth thick porridge.
2. Heat sesame oil in a pot and fry ginger, garlic and prawns together until prawns begin to change colour.
3. Add hot porridge, salt and soy sauce and bring to the boil.
4. Garnish with chopped spring onions and sesame salt to taste.
5. Serve hot with pickled vegetables or kimchi.

TIP
For a Thai flavour, serve the porridge with a vinegar-chilli dip (page 10) or red chillies with fish sauce (page 15) and a wedge of lime.

Ogokpap (Korean Five-grain Rice)

Preparation time: 1 hour   Serves 3–4

Five-grain, six-grain and even seven-grain rice is common in East Asia and packages of rice mixed with other grains are now found in many supermarkets especially those with Korean or Japanese patronage. The rule with mixed-grain rice is to cook until the hardest grain in the mixture is done. This recipe includes very hard-to-cook beans, so pre-cook these first in a slow cooker overnight.

Short-grain rice	50 g (1^2/$_3$ oz / ^{1}/$_4$ cup)
Glutinous rice	50 g (1^2/$_3$ oz / ^{1}/$_4$ cup)
Barley	50 g (1^2/$_3$ oz / ^{1}/$_4$ cup), softened in cold water
Brown rice	50 g (1^2/$_3$ oz / ^{1}/$_4$ cup), softened in cold water
Dried corn	50 g (1^2/$_3$ oz / ^{1}/$_4$ cup), softened in cold water
Water	750 ml (24 fl oz / 3 cups)
Pre-cooked black/red beans	100 g (3^1/$_2$ oz / ^{1}/$_2$ cup)
Ginger	5-cm (2-in) knob, peeled and smashed
Salt	^{1}/$_2$ tsp
Sesame oil	1 Tbsp
Chopped spring onions	to taste
Pickled vegetables (page 25) or kimchi (optional)	

GARNISH

Korean sesame salt (page 17) or *shichimi togarashi* (page 16)

1. Combine all ingredients except sesame oil and spring onions in a pot and bring to the boil. Lower heat and simmer until ingredients are tender and grains are fairly dry.
2. Stir in sesame oil and spring onions.
3. Serve warm or cold with pickled vegetables or kimchi. Garnish with Korean sesame salt or *shichimi togarashi*.

Turkish Aubergine and Tomato Pilaf

Preparation time: 45 minutes   Serves 3–4

This vegetarian pilaf is simple enough for an everyday meal but can be dressed with a grilled meat or meat stew for a more festive meal. To make a more complete meal, add boiled chickpeas or lentils to it. Or serve it with a yoghurt sauce or raita.

Aubergines	500 g (1 lb 1^1/$_2$ oz)
Olive oil	4 Tbsp
Onions	100 g (3^1/$_2$ oz), peeled and thinly sliced or cubed
Long-grain rice	250 g (9 oz / 1^1/$_4$ cups / 1^2/$_3$ rice cooker cups)
Boiled chickpeas (optional)	100 g (3^1/$_2$ oz / ^{1}/$_2$ cup)
Tomatoes	200 g (7 oz), thickly sliced
Salt	1^1/$_2$ tsp
Water	625 ml (20 fl oz / 2^1/$_2$ cups)
Cooked yoghurt sauce (page 19), cucumber raita (page 18) or pickled vegetables (page 25) (optional)	

1. Cut aubergines into thick slices with the skin on. Heat a cast-iron frying pan, brush the pan lightly with oil and brown aubergine slices on both sides.

2. Heat olive oil in a wok and brown onions. Stir in browned aubergines and mix well. Sauté until aubergines are just soft.

3. Combine rice, boiled chickpeas, if using, tomatoes, salt and water and cook rice using your preferred method.

4. When rice is done, fluff it up and scoop out three-quarters from the cooking pot. Spoon in half the aubergine slices and cover with half the scooped-out rice. Top that layer with the remaining aubergine slices and cover with the remainder of the rice. Let rice rest for 10 minutes before serving.

5. Serve with cooked yoghurt sauce, cucumber raita or pickled vegetables.

Puliyodarai (South Indian Tamarind Rice)

Preparation time: 30 minutes–2 hours   Serves 3–4

This can be a quick dish if you use tinned boiled chickpeas or have some in the freezer. (I usually increase the amount of chickpeas that I boil and freeze what I don't need for another day.) You can also drop the chickpeas and use just the quick-cooking dhals like mung or masoor. Both these dhals usually take less than 30 minutes to soften if pre-soaked.

Ghee/cooking oil	3 Tbsp
Hot cooked long-grain rice	3 cups (from 225 g / 8 oz / 1$\frac{1}{2}$ rice cooker cups rice)
Indian garam masala (page 12)	1 Tbsp
White sesame seeds	1 Tbsp
Chilli powder	1 Tbsp
Tamarind paste	75 g (2$\frac{1}{2}$ oz)
Water	1 litre (32 fl oz / 4 cups)
Curry leaves	1 sprig
Mustard seeds	2 tsp
Onion	50 g (1$\frac{2}{3}$ oz / $\frac{1}{4}$ cup), peeled and thinly sliced
Mung beans/masoor dhal	100 g (3$\frac{1}{2}$ oz / $\frac{1}{2}$ cup), soaked 1 hour
Boiled chickpeas (chana dhal)	3 cups
Salt	1$\frac{1}{2}$ tsp
Sugar	to taste

GARNISH
Toasted cashew nuts (page 10)
Chopped mint leaves

1. Stir 1 Tbsp ghee/oil into hot cooked rice together with $\frac{1}{2}$ tsp garam masala and keep rice warm.

2. Dry-fry sesame seeds to brown them but take care not to burn them. Pound to release oils. Set aside.

3. Mix remainder of garam masala and chilli powder together with some water to form a thick paste.

4. Mix tamarind paste with 1 litre (32 fl oz / 4 cups) water and strain away solids. Set aside tamarind juice until needed.

5. Heat remaining 2 Tbsp ghee/oil in a wok and fry curry leaves and mustard seeds together until mustard seeds pop. Add onion and garam masala paste and stir-fry until fragrant.

6. Add tamarind juice, soaked mung beans/masoor dhal, boiled chickpeas and salt and simmer gently until dhal is tender. There should be at least 750 ml (24 fl oz / 3 cups) thick gravy in the stew. Stir in sugar to taste and sesame seeds when dhal is cooked.

7. To serve, dish out rice onto a serving dish and top with dhal dressing. (Note that if dressing is left to cool down, it will thicken. If so, stir in some water or tamarind juice to thin it out again.)

8. Garnish with cashew nuts and mint leaves.

West Asian Mushroom Pilaf

Preparation time: 1 hour   Serves 3–4

This mushroom pilaf gets its light sour touch from sumac. However, if sumac is not available, serve the pilaf with a small bowl of lime or lemon juice to be added to taste and stirred into the rice. Another way is to serve the pilaf with a yoghurt sauce.

Olive oil	3 Tbsp
Onion	100 g (3$^1/_2$ oz), peeled and finely chopped
Garlic	3 cloves, peeled and chopped
Tomatoes	250 g (9 oz), skinned and chopped
Capsicum	1, seeded and sliced into strips
Salt	1$^1/_2$ tsp
Baharat (page 12)	1$^1/_2$ tsp
Fresh mushrooms	500 g (1 lb 1$^1/_2$ oz), cleaned and thickly sliced
Long-grain rice	250 g (9 oz / 1$^1/_4$ cups / 1$^2/_3$ rice cooker cups)
Water	625 ml (20 fl oz / 2$^1/_2$ cups)
Cooked yoghurt sauce (page 19) or yoghurt dip (page 19)	
Pickled vegetables (page 25) (optional)	

GARNISH

Sumac or lime/lemon juice	to taste
Chopped mint/coriander leaves	to taste

1. Heat olive oil in a frying pan and fry onion and garlic until fragrant. Add tomatoes, capsicum, $^1/_2$ tsp salt and baharat and fry for 2 minutes until tomatoes begin to dry out. Stir in mushrooms and mix well to coat mushrooms with tomatoes and spices. Heat mushrooms through but do not boil.

2. Combine rice with water and remaining salt and cook rice using your preferred method. When rice is done, fluff it up and stir in mushroom mixture. Cover and rest rice for 10 minutes before serving.

3. Before serving rice, mix in sumac or lime/lemon juice and garnish with chopped mint/coriander leaves.

4. Serve with cooked yoghurt sauce or yoghurt dip and pickled vegetables.

TIP

To clean mushrooms, wipe each mushroom gently with paper towels. Trim off and discard the stems.

Rice with Spinach, West Asian-style

Preparation time: 45 minutes   Serves 3–4

If you can get pre-washed baby spinach, fixing this dish is a snap. Otherwise, cleaning spinach (also called *bayam* in Malay) is tedious. Not only do you have to get rid of the coarse stems and tough leaves, you also have to strip off the tough thin membrane that covers the stems. All this reduces a kilo of spinach by nearly half. Fresh spinach should be well-rinsed in several changes of cold water to get rid of grit. The cooking time depends on the kind of spinach, with baby spinach being fairly quick.

Long-grain rice	250 g (9 oz / 1¼ cups / 1⅔ rice cooker cups)
Water	625 ml (20 fl oz / 2½ cups)
Olive oil/ghee	3 Tbsp
Advieh/baharat (page 12)	1 tsp
Salt	1½ tsp
Onions	100 g (3½ oz), peeled and thinly sliced
Garlic	2 cloves, peeled and thinly sliced
Spinach	750 g (1 lb 11 oz), cleaned and coarsely chopped

GARNISH AND CONDIMENTS
Lemon wedges/sumac
Cooked yoghurt sauce
  (page 19) or yoghurt dip
  (page 19)

1. Cook rice with water, 2 Tbsp olive oil/ghee, advieh/baharat and 1 tsp salt using your preferred method.

2. Heat remaining olive oil/ghee in a saucepan big enough to contain cooked rice. Fry onions until fragrant and as the onions begin to brown, add garlic. Continue frying until garlic is a pale golden colour. Stir in remaining ½ tsp salt and spinach and fry until spinach changes colour. If using baby spinach, turn off heat now. If not, simmer for a couple of minutes until spinach is nearly at preferred texture. The spinach should be moist but not swimming in liquid.

3. When rice is done, fluff it up and transfer to the saucepan. Press rice down gently so it takes the shape of the saucepan.

4. Cover saucepan with a clean dishcloth wrapped around the lid or with several layers of paper towels and the lid clamped on tightly. Have the heat on very low to infuse the flavours for 10 minutes.

5. The spinach and rice can also be baked in an ovenproof dish in a 160°C (325°F) oven for 20 minutes. Divide the rice and spinach into two oven-proof dishes if you don't have a large enough ovenproof dish.

6. To serve, turn rice out onto a deep-dish platter so that spinach is on top of rice.

7. Serve with lemon wedges or a dish of sumac powder and cooked yoghurt sauce or yoghurt dip.

Tamatar Pulao (Indian Tomato Rice)

Preparation time: 30 minutes   Serves 3–4

This pilaf is usually made with skinned tomatoes. Use canned tomatoes to speed up the process. If using fresh tomatoes, leave them unpeeled.

Ghee	2 Tbsp
Garlic	2 cloves, peeled and finely ground
Ginger	5-cm (2-in) knob, peeled and finely chopped
Tomatoes or canned tomatoes	300 g (11 oz), chopped
Green chillies	2, seeded and coarsely chopped
Salt	1 1/2 tsp
Ground cumin	1/2 tsp
Indian bay leaves	2
Basmati rice	250 g (9 oz / 1 1/4 cups / 1 2/3 rice cooker cups)
Water	as needed

GARNISH AND CONDIMENTS

Chopped coriander leaves

Chopped spring onions

Toasted cashew nuts (page 10)

Pickled vegetables (page 25), cucumber raita (page 18) or cooked yoghurt sauce (page 19)

1. Heat ghee in a pot and fry garlic and ginger until fragrant. Add tomatoes, chillies, salt, cumin and bay leaves and fry for 2 minutes.

2. Add enough water to mixture to get 750 ml (24 fl oz / 3 cups) liquid. Combine this mixture with rice and cook rice using your preferred method. When rice is done, fluff it up and stir down the ingredients. Cover and rest rice for another 10 minutes.

3. Before serving rice, mix in chopped coriander and spring onions and garnish with toasted cashew nuts.

4. Serve pilaf with pickled vegetables, cucumber raita or cooked yoghurt sauce.

Kedgeree (Indian Dhal Rice)

Preparation time: 1 hour   Serves 3–4

Use any quick-cooking dhal such as mung dhal or masoor dhal for this dish. Mung dhal is skinned, split mung beans while masoor dhal is the distinctive reddish-pink dhal. However, note that dhal or beans that have been stored for a long time take longer to cook than fresher dhal.

Ghee/cooking oil	2 Tbsp
Mustard seeds	1 tsp
Onion	50 g (1²/₃ oz), peeled and thinly sliced
Ginger	5-cm (2-in) knob, peeled and chopped
Tomatoes	100 g (3¹/₂ oz), diced
Dhal	200 g (7 oz / 1 cup), soaked for 30 minutes
Salt	1¹/₂ tsp
Water	1 litre (32 fl oz /4 cups)
Long-grain rice	250 g (9 oz / 1¹/₄ cups / 1²/₃ rice cooker cups)
Indian garam masala (page 12)	¹/₂ tsp

GARNISH AND CONDIMENTS (OPTIONAL)
Chopped coriander leaves
Cucumber raita (page 18)
  or pickled vegetables (page 25)

1. In a saucepan, heat 1 Tbsp ghee/oil and fry mustard seeds until they pop. Pour into a small bowl and set aside.

2. Using the same pan, heat remaining ghee/oil and fry onion and ginger until pale brown and fragrant. Add tomatoes, dhal, ¹/₂ tsp salt, and 1 litre (32 fl oz / 4 cups) water and bring to the boil. Lower heat and simmer until dhal is nearly tender and still whole.

3. Pour dhal liquid into a measuring cup and top up with water to get 625 ml (20 fl oz / 2¹/₂ cups) liquid if necessary. Cook the rice with this liquid, with remaining salt and dhal added, using your preferred method.

4. When rice is done, fluff it up and stir in garam masala, mustard seeds and chopped coriander leaves, if using. Rest rice for 10 minutes before serving.

5. Serve hot with cucumber raita or pickled vegetables.

Thai Fried Rice Salad

Preparation time: 30 minutes   Serves 3–4

In the 1980s, cooked food stalls in Thailand always served fried rice with a plate of greens, wedges of lime and lengths of spring onions. These days, fried rice does not always come with raw vegetables or even lime wedges. I wonder why. Too many tourists refusing to eat raw vegetables?

Cooking oil	2 Tbsp
Chopped garlic	1 Tbsp
Peeled prawns/sliced pork/ beef shreds/firm bean curd	200 g (7 oz)
Fish sauce	2 Tbsp
Cold cooked long-grain rice	3 cups (prepared using 225 g / 8 oz / 1$^1/_2$ rice cooker cups rice)
Basil	$^1/_2$ cup
Coriander leaves	1 large bunch, chopped
Red chillies with fish sauce (page 15)	

GARNISH

Spring onions	8, large
Cabbage	200 g (7 oz), cut into wedges
Cucumbers	200 g (7 oz), cut into long strips
Large limes	2, cut into wedges

1. Heat oil in a wok and fry garlic until fragrant. Add prawns/meat/bean curd, with 1 Tbsp fish sauce and fry until prawns change colour or meat is cooked. Stir in rice and remainder of fish sauce. Mix well and fry until rice is heated through.

2. Stir in basil and coriander leaves. Dish rice out into individual serving plates.

3. Trim roots from spring onions and keep it in long lengths. Arrange spring onions on a plate with cabbage, cucumbers and limes.

4. Serve rice with the plate of garnish and red chillies with fish sauce on the side. Squeeze lime juice over fried rice to taste, stir in chillies and fish sauce and enjoy the rice with bites of raw vegetables and spring onion.

Yong Chew Fried Rice (Yangzhou Fried Rice)

Preparation time: 1 hour   Serves 3–4

One way to get every grain of rice a delicate yellow is to coat the cold rice in an egg wash before you fry it at high heat. The coated rice has to be fried in small batches over high heat. So have all ingredients ready to pop into the pan before the wok is heated up.

Cold cooked long-grain rice	3 cups (from 225 g / 8 oz / 1$^1/_2$ rice cooker cups rice)
Sesame oil	1$^1/_2$ Tbsp
Ground white pepper	$^1/_2$ tsp
Salt	1 tsp
Eggs	4, beaten
Cooking oil	4 Tbsp
Small peeled prawns	100 g (3$^1/_2$ oz)
Carrot	100 g (3$^1/_2$ oz), peeled and cubed small
Green peas	100 g (3$^1/_2$ oz)
Chinese-style red roast pork (page 22)	100 g (3$^1/_2$ oz), cubed small
Spring onion	1, large, chopped

1. In a mixing bowl, prepare rice by coating it well with sesame oil, pepper and salt.
2. Stir half the beaten eggs into the cold rice.
3. Heat oil in a wok and fry prawns until they change colour. Dish out and set aside.
4. Reheat oil until very hot, then pour in remaining beaten eggs and let a layer set before adding the egg-coated rice. Stir-fry quickly to break up the layer of egg and to set the egg-wash on the rice.
5. Add carrot, green peas, roast pork and prawns in that order. Stir-fry for a couple of minutes, then add spring onion.
6. Dish out and serve hot.

Teochew Olive Rice

Preparation time: 20 minutes   Serves 4–5

A Teochew speciality, bottled *kana chye*, a salted vegetable pickled with Chinese olives in oil, is delicious fried with rice. It is so tasty that it has a place in Thai restaurant menus. Because the olives in bottled *kana chye* are often pickled with the seeds, they have to be seeded. Use the tasty pickling oil for frying the rice.

Bottled *kana chye* (olive vegetables)	3 Tbsp
Olive oil (optional)	1–2 Tbsp
Chopped garlic	1 Tbsp
Peeled prawns	200 g (7 oz)
Cold cooked long-grain rice	3 cups (from 225 g / 8 oz / 1$^1/_2$ rice cooker cups rice)
Dark soy sauce	2–3 drops
Chopped spring onions	1 cup
Coriander leaves	1 small bunch, chopped
Chinese-style chicken vegetable soup (page 23)	

1. Scoop out vegetables and olives from bottled *kana chye*. Using two spoons, squeeze out the oil into a wok. Add a spoonful of olive oil if there is insufficient oil for frying.
2. Seed olives and cut into thin wedges or rings. The vegetable requires no preparation.
3. Heat oil and fry garlic until fragrant, then add prawns and sauté until they change colour.
4. Stir in rice, *kana chye* and a few drops dark soy sauce to colour rice. Fry until rice is heated through, then stir in chopped spring onions and coriander leaves.
5. Serve hot with a soup.

Beef Fried Rice

Preparation time: 30 minutes   Serves 3–4

This delicious fried rice is one of my favourite ways of enjoying beef. It makes good use of a cheap cut of meat.

Rump steak	300 g (11 oz)
Bicarbonate of soda	$1/4$ tsp
Light soy sauce	1 Tbsp
Dark soy sauce	1 tsp
Ground white pepper	$1/2$ tsp
Cooking oil	3 Tbsp
Shallots	100 g ($3^1/2$ oz), peeled and thinly sliced
Cold cooked long-grain rice	3 cups (from 225 g / 8 oz / $1^1/2$ rice cooker cups rice)
Salt	$1/2$ tsp

GARNISH AND CONDIMENT

Coriander leaves	1 large bunch, chopped
Red chillies with soy sauce (page 15)	

1. Trim off any fat and gristle from meat, then slice thinly across the grain and marinate with bicarbonate of soda, $1/2$ Tbsp light soy sauce, $1/2$ tsp dark soy sauce and $1/4$ tsp pepper. Cover and refrigerate for 1 hour.

2. Heat oil in a wok and fry shallots until it begins to colour. Stir in beef and after 1 minute, add rice, salt, remaining pepper, and soy sauces. Fry for a few minutes to cook beef and heat rice through. Do not overcook beef. Fry on high heat so that rice will be dry.

3. Stir in coriander leaves last.

4. Serve hot with a condiment of red chillies with soy sauce on the side.

Kimchi Fried Rice

Preparation time: 30 minutes   Serves 3–4

This rice tastes great whether fried with cooked long-grain or short-grain rice. To avoid getting soggy rice, squeeze the kimchi very dry before cutting it up. Save the pickling liquid for making kimchi soup (page 54) to go with the rice. If perilla leaves are cheaply available, serve the fried rice with perilla leaves for wrapping the rice. Or use lettuce leaves as wraps and with added slivers of raw garlic for more punch.

Kimchi	400 g (14$\frac{1}{3}$ oz / 2 cups)
Cooking oil	3 Tbsp
Garlic	6 cloves, peeled and chopped
Peeled prawns/chicken/ pork slivers	200 g (7 oz)
Salt	1 tsp
Red chilli	1, sliced
Cold cooked short-grain/ long-grain rice	3 cups (from 225 g / 8 oz / 1$\frac{1}{2}$ rice cooker cups rice)
Sesame oil	1 Tbsp

GARNISH
Chopped spring onions
Chopped coriander leaves

1. Dry kimchi by squeezing juices into a bowl, then cut into thin slices.
2. Heat cooking oil in a wok and sauté half the chopped garlic until fragrant, but not brown. Stir in prawns/chicken/pork into hot oil and fry until prawns change colour or meat is cooked.
3. Add kimchi, salt and chilli and mix well. Fry for 1 minute, then add rice, sesame oil and remaining raw garlic and fry until rice is heated through.
4. Stir in chopped spring onions and coriander leaves.

Oyster Sauce Fried Rice

Preparation time: 30 minutes   Serves 3–4

Cold cooked rice or noodles fried with oyster sauce makes a tasty dish. You can make it vegetarian by substituting firm bean curd for prawns and using vegetarian oyster sauce instead of regular oyster sauce.

Cooking oil	3 Tbsp
Garlic	6, peeled and chopped
Red chillies	3, seeded and thinly sliced
Peeled prawns	300 g (11 oz)
Cabbage	500 g (1 lb 1½ oz), shredded
Oyster sauce	3 Tbsp
Salt	1 tsp
Ground white pepper	1 tsp
Cold cooked long-grain rice	3 cups (from 225 g / 8 oz / 1½ rice cooker cups rice)

GARNISH

Chopped spring onions

Lime halves/lemon wedges
  (optional)

1. Heat oil in a wok and sauté garlic and chillies until fragrant, then add prawns and cabbage. Fry until prawns begin to change colour.
2. Stir in oyster sauce, salt and pepper and mix well, then stir in rice and fry until heated through.
3. Lastly, stir in chopped spring onions.
4. Dish out and garnish each serving with lime halves/lemon wedges.

Nasi Goreng (Malay/Straits Chinese Fried Rice)

Preparation time: 30 minutes   Serves 3–4

Adding vegetables to *nasi goreng* makes it a complete meal. At the same time, the vegetables add colour and crunch. Carrots or green beans are particularly good.

Cooking oil	3 Tbsp
Onion	75 g (2²/₃ oz), peeled and cubed small
Green beans/carrots	200 g (7 oz)
Peeled prawns/chicken/beef	200 g (7 oz)
Sambal belacan (page 13)	1 Tbsp
Salt	³/₄ tsp
Cold cooked long-grain rice	3 cups (from 225 g / 8 oz / 1¹/₂ rice cooker cups rice)

GARNISH
Chopped spring onions

1. Heat oil in a wok and fry onion until it begins to colour. Stir in vegetable first, then prawns/meat and fry until prawns begin to change colour or meat is nearly cooked. If using beef, take care not to overcook beef.

2. Before prawns or meat is cooked, add *sambal belacan* and fry for another minute or so, then stir in salt and rice and heat through.

3. Stir in chopped spring onions last. Serve hot.

Indonesian Nasi Goreng (Indonesian Fried Rice)

Preparation time: 1 hour   Serves 3–4

Indonesian *nasi goreng* seems to always include two sticks of succulent satay. As satay is time-consuming to prepare, a quick alternative is to do a simple fried chicken seasoned with salt and pepper or grill the satay using a stove-top grill. (Another essential with Indonesian fried rice are the pieces of crisp prawn crackers which were forgotten during photography!)

Boneless chicken	300 g (11 oz), cubed
Bamboo skewers	12
Cooking oil	5 Tbsp
Onions	100 g (3¹/₂ oz), peeled and cubed
Bottled *sambal oelek* or chilli paste (recipe below)	4 Tbsp
Peeled small prawns	200 g (7 oz)
Salt	1 tsp
Cold cooked long-grain rice	3 cups (from 225 g / 8 oz / 1¹/₂ rice cooker cups rice)
Eggs	1 per serving
Fried prawn crackers	a few pieces per serving

MARINADE FOR CHICKEN

Indonesian sweet dark soy sauce (*kicap manis*)	2 tsp
Lemon grass	1 stalk, thinly sliced and finely ground
Ground coriander	1 tsp
Cooking oil	1 Tbsp
Salt	1 tsp
Sugar	2 Tbsp

CHILLI PASTE (OPTIONAL)

Red chillies	3, seeded
Shallots	3, peeled and chopped
Dried prawn paste (*belacan*)	¹/₂ tsp
Sugar	¹/₂ tsp

1. Mix chicken with marinade and stand for a few hours or overnight. Divide into 12 portions and thread meat through bamboo skewers. Start grilling satay before frying rice. The two tasks should be finished at about the same time so satay and rice can be enjoyed while hot. When grilling satay, brush oil on meat to keep it moist.

2. If *sambal oelek* is not available, make chilli paste. Pound ingredients together until fine. Alternatively, blend in a food processor with some water. Set aside.

3. Heat 3 Tbsp oil in a wok and fry onions until they begin to soften. Add *sambal oelek* or chilli paste, prawns and salt and fry until prawns change colour. Stir in rice and mix well, heating rice through. Turn off heat and keep rice warm.

4. In a frying pan, heat ¹/₂ Tbsp oil and fry eggs one at a time sunny-side up or according to individual taste.

5. Serve rice on individual plates topped with a fried egg, 2–3 sticks of satay and prawn crackers.

Rice with Lime Dressing, Indian-style

Preparation time: 30 minutes   Serves 3–4

Do a taste test when making this dressing as you may prefer it more or less tart. While fresh white grated coconut (the kind without the brown skin) is best, you can also use canned desiccated coconut provided it has not been flavoured. Plump up the desiccated coconut with some water before mixing with the other ingredients. Unlike fried rice, this dressed rice is made with hot rice.

Long-grain rice	250 g (9 oz / 1¼ cups / 1⅔ rice cooker cups)
Water	625 ml (20 fl oz / 2½ cups)
Salt	1½ tsp
Ground turmeric	¼ tsp
Ghee/cooking oil	2 Tbsp
Ginger	10 thin slices, finely shredded
Chilli powder	1 tsp
Boiled chickpeas	3 cups
Fresh grated coconut without skin	½ cup
Finely grated lime zest	1 tsp
Green chillies	2, seeded and thinly sliced
Lime juice	2 Tbsp
Cooked yoghurt sauce (page 19) or cucumber raita (page 18)	

GARNISH

Chopped coriander leaves

Toasted cashew nuts/ almonds/peanuts

1. Combine rice, water, 1 tsp salt and turmeric and cook rice using your preferred method. While rice is cooking, prepare the dressing.

2. Heat ghee/oil in a wok and add ginger, chilli powder, boiled chickpeas and remaining ½ tsp salt. Stir-fry, smashing up some of the chickpeas.

3. Stir in grated coconut and lime zest and use the spatula to turn the ingredients constantly until coconut is dry. If using desiccated coconut and it is very dry, plump it up with some water or lime juice during the frying.

4. Stir in green chillies and lime juice. Mix well. Adjust seasoning to taste. Divide dressing between servings of warm rice. Garnish with chopped coriander leaves and toasted nuts.

5. Serve with cooked yoghurt sauce or cucumber raita.

Indian-style Pea Pulao

Preparation time: 30 minutes   Serves 3–4

Fresh peas are common in Indian markets and these peas are delicious cooked with rice because Indian fresh peas are picked when mature and keep their texture well. While fresh green peas are not found in Singapore wet markets, there are fresh streaky beans which make an excellent substitute for fresh green peas. Like peas, they take about the same time to soften as rice and have a cooked texture similar to Indian peas.

Ghee	3 Tbsp
Ginger	6 slices, finely shredded
Garlic	1 clove, peeled and finely chopped
Tomatoes	200 g (7 oz), skinned and coarsely chopped
Fresh green peas	300 g (11 oz / 1^1/$_2$ cups)
Salt	1^1/$_2$ tsp
Long-grain rice	250 g (9 oz / 1^1/$_4$ cups / 1^2/$_3$ rice cooker cups)
Water	625 ml (20 fl oz / 2^1/$_2$ cups)
Cucumber raita (page 18), cooked yoghurt sauce (page 19) or pickled vegetables (page 25)	

GARNISH
Chopped coriander leaves/mint

1. Heat ghee in a frying pan and fry ginger and garlic until fragrant but not brown. Add tomatoes and peas and stir-fry for 5 minutes to soften tomatoes. Stir in salt.
2. Combine tomato and pea mixture with rice and water and cook rice using your preferred method.
3. Before serving, stir chopped herb of choice into hot rice.
4. Serve with cucumber raita, cooked yoghurt sauce or pickled vegetables.

Kuri Gohan (Japanese Chestnut Rice)

Preparation time: 45 minutes   Serves 3–4

The smell of roasting sweet chestnuts fill the air in autumn in East Asia when this nut appears in profusion in markets. Sweet chestnuts are delicious in soups, stews and rice dumplings and in Japan, these chestnuts are cooked with rice to make *kuri gohan*.

Fresh sweet chestnuts	300 g (11 oz)
Short-grain rice	250 g (9 oz / 1¼ cups / 1⅔ rice cooker cups)
Mirin	2 Tbsp
Ginger	6 thin slices, peeled and finely shredded
Water	625 ml (20 fl oz / 2½ cups)
Shichimi togarashi (page 16) or Korean sesame salt (page 17)	to taste
Green spring onion tips	to taste, finely chopped
Pickled vegetables (page 25)	
Wasabi	to taste
Light soy sauce	to taste

1. If using chestnuts that have not been shelled, cut into the soft stiff shell with a small paring knife and peel it off. To remove the thin papery skin, boil the nuts in water for 10 minutes, then peel off loosened skins. Quarter chestnuts if they are large.

2. Combine rice, mirin, ginger and chestnuts with water and cook rice using your preferred method. When rice is done, fluff it up and rest rice for 10 minutes before serving.

3. Dish rice out into rice bowls. Sprinkle some *shichimi togarashi* or Korean sesame salt and green spring onion tips on top.

4. Serve with pickled vegetables and a condiment of wasabi and light soy sauce.

Kongnamulpap (Korean Rice with Soy Bean Sprouts and Beef)

Preparation time: 30 minutes   Serves 3–4

Soy bean sprouts are distinguished from mung bean sprouts by the much larger yellow head. Soy bean sprouts are sometimes sold tied in convenient bundles. Cut off the tails with a knife. Substitute soy bean sprouts with mung bean sprouts or any other sprouts if soy bean sprouts are not easily available. If using more delicate sprouts, just stir them into the cooked rice before topping with cooked beef. The beef can be substituted with pork or chicken if preferred.

Short-grain rice	250 g (9 oz / $1^1/_4$ cups / $1^2/_3$ rice cooker cups)
Water	625 ml (20 fl oz / $2^1/_2$ cups)
Cooking oil	2 Tbsp
Soy bean sprouts	300 g (11 oz), tailed
Kimchi or pickled vegetables (page 25)	

MEAT AND MARINADE

Shredded beef/pork/chicken	200 g (7 oz)
Ginger	4 slices, peeled and finely shredded
Sesame oil	1 Tbsp
Light soy sauce	1 Tbsp
Sugar	1 tsp
Salt	1 tsp

GARNISH

Chopped spring onions

Korean sesame salt (page 17)
  or *shichimi togarashi*
  (page 16)

1. Mix meat and marinade together and stand while rice is cooking or leave overnight in the fridge in a covered container.
2. Cook rice with water using your preferred method. If using leftover rice, steam it well to fluff it up.
3. Heat oil and fry marinated meat for 1 minute over high heat. Add bean sprouts and fry for another minute. Fluff up rice and stir meat and sprouts into it.
4. Garnish with chopped spring onions and a sprinkling of Korean sesame salt or *shichimi togarashi*.
5. Serve hot with kimchi or pickled vegetables.

Khao Phad Prik Khing (Thai Fried Curried Rice)

Preparation time: 30 minutes   Serves 3–4

Use packaged Thai curry paste such as red or green curry paste. Note though that packaged curry paste tends to be rather salty, so do a taste test before adding the fish sauce.

Cooking oil	3 Tbsp
Packaged red/green curry paste	2 Tbsp
Chicken/pork/beef	300 g (11 oz), thinly sliced, or peeled prawns
Long beans/French beans/carrots	300 g (11 oz), cut into short finger lengths, or peas
Cold cooked long-grain rice	3 cups (from 225 g / 8 oz / 1½ rice cooker cups rice)
Kaffir lime leaves	3, crushed
Fish sauce	2 Tbsp

GARNISH
Chopped coriander leaves
Lime wedges

1. Heat oil in a wok and fry spice paste until fragrant and oil surfaces before adding meat or prawns. Fry until meat is cooked or prawns change colour before adding chosen vegetable. Mix well and fry for 1–2 minutes. The vegetables should still be crisp.

2. Add rice, crushed lime leaves and do a taste test before adding any fish sauce. Mix well and continue frying to heat the rice through.

3. Garnish with coriander leaves and lime wedges.

Japanese Red Bean Rice

Preparation time: 1 hour   Serves 3–4

This is a quick dish to prepare. The sticky short-grain rice can be shaped into balls or triangles, then wrapped with strips of seaweed to make for easier handling. Alternatively, press the rice into a lunch box and eat with chopsticks. Wasabi is sold in tubes in Asian supermarkets.

White short-grain rice	250 g (9 oz / 1$\frac{1}{4}$ cups / 1$\frac{2}{3}$ rice cooker cups)
Pre-cooked or canned adzuki beans	100 g (3$\frac{1}{2}$ oz / $\frac{1}{2}$ cup)
Ginger	4 slices, finely shredded
Water	625 ml (20 fl oz / 2$\frac{1}{2}$ cups)
Japanese vinegar	1 Tbsp
Spring onion	1, just the green tip, finely chopped
Korean sesame salt (page 17) or *shichimi togarashi* (page 16)	

FOR MAKING RICE BALLS (OPTIONAL)

Muslin cloth moistened with
  Japanese vinegar

Nori sheets

1. Combine rice with adzuki beans, ginger and water and cook rice using your preferred method. When rice is done, stir in vinegar and spring onion.

2. Sprinkle some Korean sesame salt or *shichimi togarashi* on top before serving.

3. To make rice balls, divide the rice into 12–14 portions. Put a portion of rice on the muslin cloth and roll the rice into a ball or shape into a triangle or a roll. To get finger food, wrap the balls with strips of nori. Garnish and serve rice balls with wasabi and light soy sauce and pickled vegetables (page 25).

Ochazuke (Rice in Green Tea)

Preparation time: 10 minutes, using leftovers

While the Chinese fry leftover rice, the Japanese will typically pour hot green tea over their leftover rice and garnish it with whatever cooked leftovers may be in the fridge. However, do not use raw or smoked seafood. The freshly-made green tea will heat up the leftovers somewhat but it is best to warm the leftovers briefly in a microwave oven first.

Cooked chicken/fish
Cooked short-grain rice
Shredded ginger
Grilled, shredded nori
Chopped perilla/spring onions
Freshly-made green tea
Korean sesame salt (page 17) or
   shichimi togarashi (page 16)
Pickled vegetables (page 25)

1. Shred or flake chicken/fish. Put chicken/fish with rice, shredded ginger, shredded nori and chopped herb in a rice bowl. Heat briefly in the microwave oven.

2. Pour freshly-made hot green tea over mixture.

3. Serve with Korean sesame salt or *shichimi togarashi* and a dish of pickled vegetables, Japanese if possible.

Chirashi-zushi

Preparation time: 30 minutes   Serves 3–4

Chirashi-zushi is casual family fare made in the *hangiri* and brought to the table. The *hangiri* is a wooden container used specially to mix vinegar into hot rice for sushi-making. Everything goes on top of the vinegared rice including the vegetable pickles, seaweed strips and seafood. The seafood can consist of raw or cooked fish. The quantity is easily tailored to suit the numbers. Japanese and other Asian supermarkets sell ready-to-use grilled seaweed called nori in sizes that range from fine strips to large sheets for wrapping sushi. If you already have nori sheets for making sushi or even snack packs of nori, simply cut a few sheets into thin strips for the garnish.

Short-grain rice	250 g (9 oz / 1$\frac{1}{4}$ cups / 1$\frac{2}{3}$ rice cooker cups)
Water	625 ml (20 fl oz / 2$\frac{1}{2}$ cups)
Cooking oil for frying	
Egg	1, beaten
Japanese vinegar	2 Tbsp
Raw/cooked seafood	200 g (7 oz)
Seasoned vegetables/seaweed	2 cups
Wasabi	to taste
Light soy sauce	to taste
GARNISH	
Green tips of spring onions	to taste, finely cut
Finely cut nori strips	to taste

1. Combine rice and water and cook rice using your preferred method.
2. While rice is cooking, heat oil in a frying pan and fry egg into 2–3 thin omelettes. Roll up and slice thinly.
3. When rice is cooked, fluff it up and spoon it into a *hangiri*. Mix vinegar into hot rice using quick turning movements with your rice paddle.
4. Arrange egg strips, raw/cooked seafood and seasoned vegetables/seaweed on vinegared rice. Garnish with a light sprinkling of spring onion tips and nori strips.
5. Serve with wasabi and light soy sauce.

Mui Fun (Cantonese Rice in Seafood Sauce)

Preparation time: 30 minutes   Serves 3–4

If you like your food full of sauce, this is the dish for you. The seafood can be whatever you have in the freezer.

Cooking oil	4 Tbsp
Garlic	3 cloves, peeled and chopped
Pork/chicken	100 g (3¹/₂ oz), thinly sliced
Mustard greens	400 g (14¹/₃ oz), cut into finger lengths
Peeled prawns with tails on	200 g (7 oz)
Squid	100 g (3¹/₂ oz), cleaned and cut into rings
Cooked long-grain rice	3 cups (from 225 g / 8 oz / 1¹/₂ rice cooker cups rice)
Pickled green chillies (page 25)	

SAUCE

Water	250 ml (8 fl oz / 1 cup)
Cornflour	¹/₂ Tbsp
Dark soy sauce	¹/₂ tsp
Light soy sauce	1¹/₂ Tbsp
Salt	¹/₂ tsp
Ground white pepper	¹/₂ tsp

1. Mix together ingredients for sauce in a bowl. Stir well just before adding to wok.
2. Heat oil in a wok over high heat and sauté garlic until fragrant. Stir in pork/chicken and fry until meat is cooked. Add mustard greens, then prawns and when prawns begin to change colour, add squid.
3. This step is optional. When squid begins to turn opaque, hold wok such that the oil in the wok will catch the flames. Stir vigorously as you do so. This singeing to get the *wok hei* (breath of the wok) is only possible if you cook with gas or an open fire.
4. Quickly add rice, mix well and add sauce. Bring to the bojl.
5. Serve immediately with a condiment of pickled green chillies.

Hokkien Yam Rice

Preparation time: 45 minutes   Serves 3–4

This traditional one-dish meal tastes best when what we call yam (*Colocasia esculenta*) which is also known as taro, cocoyam or dasheen elsewhere, is fluffy (like a Russet potato). An old-fashioned test that a wet market stallholder would use to check if the yam will be fluffy is to slice a thin piece from the bottom of the yam. If a powdery white residue forms on the blade, the yam is supposed to be fluffy. However, I have found that the small tubby Thai yams are almost always fluffy compared to the larger Chinese yams when it can be hit and miss.

Cooking oil	3 Tbsp
Garlic	1 clove, peeled and chopped
Dried prawns	2 Tbsp, finely chopped
Minced pork/chicken (optional)	100 g (3^1/$_2$ oz)
Yam	500 g (1 lb 1^1/$_2$ oz), peeled and cubed
Salt	1^1/$_2$ tsp
Long-grain rice	250 g (9 oz / 1^1/$_4$ cups / 1^2/$_3$ rice cooker cups)
Water	750 ml (24 fl oz / 3 cups)
Pickled vegetables (page 25)	

GARNISH
Chopped spring onions
Chopped coriander leaves

1. Heat oil in a wok and sauté garlic and dried prawns until fragrant.
2. Add minced meat, if using, yam, 1 tsp salt and 125 ml (4 fl oz / ^{1}/$_2$ cup) water. Mix well and cover wok. Turn down heat and simmer gently until yam is half-cooked or about 10 minutes. The time will depend on the yam and the size of the cubes. Stir occasionally to prevent yam from sticking. There should be no liquid.
3. Combine rice, yam and remaining ^{1}/$_2$ tsp salt with remaining 625 ml (20 fl oz / 2^1/$_2$ cups) water and cook rice using your preferred method. When rice is done, fluff it up gently without mashing up yam cubes too much. Rest rice for 10 minutes before serving.
4. Serve hot with a garnish of chopped spring onion and coriander leaves and pickled vegetables.

Sar Poh Fun (Cantonese Clay Pot Rice)

Preparation time: 45 minutes   Serves 3–4

Before the invention of the rice cooker, this one-dish meal would be steamed in a clay pot, a process that would have taken at least 45 minutes. There are people who insist that "clay pot" rice tastes better if steamed in a clay pot, but it is just so much easier to cook it in a rice cooker.

Dried shiitake mushrooms	4, large, softened in cold water
Boneless chicken	300 g (11 oz), cubed
Chinese sausages	2, thinly sliced
Cooking oil	2 Tbsp
Salted fish (optional)	3 thin slices, chopped or shredded
Garlic	2 cloves, peeled and chopped
Long-grain rice	250 g (9 oz / 1¼ cups / 1²/₃ rice cooker cups)
Salt	1 tsp
Water/chicken stock (page 20)	625 ml (20 fl oz / 2½ cups)
Pickled green chillies or pickled vegetables (page 25)	

CHICKEN MARINADE

Oyster sauce	2 Tbsp
Dark soy sauce	1 tsp
Sesame oil	2 tsp
Ginger	5-cm (2-in) knob, peeled and pounded to get 1 Tbsp juice

GARNISH

Chopped spring onions
Chopped coriander leaves

1. Quarter or slice mushrooms thickly according to preference. Reserve water used for soaking mushrooms for cooking rice. Measure out this water and reduce the amount of water/stock for cooking rice accordingly.

2. Combine ingredients for marinade and marinate chicken for 10 minutes.

3. In a clay pot or frying pan, if cooking the rice in a rice cooker, fry sliced Chinese sausages until oil comes out from it. Add cooking oil and stir in salted fish if using, then stir in garlic. Fry until fragrant, then add mushrooms and marinated chicken and fry for 5 minutes or so.

4. If using rice cooker, pour contents of frying pan into rice pot, add rice, salt and mushroom water and water/stock and cook as usual.

5. If using a clay pot, follow steps above but reduce water to 375 ml (12 fl oz / 1½ cups) and put everything into a clay pot and steam rice until done. Sprinkle more water over rice if it is too firm and continue steaming.

6. Serve with pickled green chillies or pickled vegetables.

Lotus Leaf-wrapped Rice

Preparation time: 45 minutes   Serves 3–4

Basically *loh mai kai* steamed in lotus leaf, this dish is good enough to serve at Chinese banquets. The salted lotus leaf imparts a special flavour to the steamed rice. Lotus leaf-wrapped rice makes a great party contribution being easy to carry around as well as easy to serve.

Lotus leaves	2–3
Twine for tying	

1. To make this dish, prepare *loh mai kai* (page 146) until step 5. Remove clay pot from steamer after 30 minutes of steaming. Divide into two or three portions depending on the size of your steamer and lotus leaf.

2. Soften the lotus leaves by blanching in boiling water or soaking for several hours in cold water until pliable. Leaves must be rinsed well but do it carefully to avoid tearing. If torn, mend it with a section of leaf from another lotus leaf.

3. Cut leaves in half, overlap two halves of a leaf and spoon a portion of rice onto the spread-out leaf. Fold into a parcel and tie with some twine. Repeat as necessary.

4. Place parcels in a steamer and steam for 30 minutes. If a softer texture is preferred, steam for longer.

5. Just before serving, use a pair of scissors and cut into the top to expose the rice.

6. Serve with a soup (page 23), stir-fried vegetables (page 24) or pickled vegetables (page 25).

Loh Mai Kai (Cantonese Glutinous Rice with Chicken)

Preparation time: 45 minutes   Serves 4–5

Loh mai kai which is a popular Cantonese dim sum item is a more fancy version of Cantonese clay pot rice. It makes a good meal by itself while leftovers make a tasty breakfast. If you have a rice cooker with a glutinous rice setting, there is no need to soak the rice at all and the glutinous rice can be cooked in the rice cooker. Without a rice cooker with a glutinous rice setting, it is best to steam the rice after soaking it in cold water for 8 hours or overnight. If steaming the rice, reduce the amount of water or stock and sprinkle water as necessary during the steaming.

Boneless chicken	200 g (7 oz), cubed
Dark soy sauce	2 tsp
Oyster sauce	2 Tbsp
Dried shiitake mushrooms	4, softened in cold water
Dried prawns (shrimps)	1 Tbsp, softened in water and chopped or 2 dried scallops, softened in water and shredded
Cooking oil	3 Tbsp
Shallots	25 g (1 oz), peeled and thinly sliced
Chinese sausage	1, thinly sliced
Leeks	150 g (5^1/$_3$ oz), thickly sliced
White glutinous rice	250 g (9 oz / 1^1/$_4$ cups / 1^2/$_3$ rice cooker cups)
Salt	^{1}/$_2$ tsp
Water	315 ml (10^1/$_2$ fl oz / 1^1/$_4$ cups) or as needed

1. Marinade chicken with dark soy sauce and oyster sauce. Cover and stand for 1 hour refrigerated.
2. Slice, quarter or halve softened mushrooms according to preference. Save water used for soaking mushrooms for cooking rice.
3. If using scallops, set aside water used for softening scallops. If using dried prawns, they can be chopped or left whole. Discard any bits of shell.
4. Heat oil in a wok and fry sliced shallots. When it begins to brown, add Chinese sausage, dried prawns or scallops and fry until shallots are golden brown. Add leeks, chicken and mushrooms and fry until chicken is almost cooked.
5. Put contents of wok into a rice cooker with a glutinous rice setting, if available, together with rice and salt. Combine mushroom and scallop water with plain cold water to get 315 ml (10^1/$_2$ fl oz / 1^1/$_4$ cups) water and add this to the rice. Cook the rice. If you do not have a rice cooker with a glutinous rice setting, reduce the water by half and put everything into a clay pot or heatproof dish and steam rice until it is done. Sprinkle in more water if necessary.
6. Dish out and serve hot.

One-dish Party Meals

One-dish party meals give your guests something to do
as well something to talk about. You supply the fixings and guests
help themselves to what they like best or make it up as they go along.

A one-dish party meal may sound like an oxymoron but in fact, quite a number of Asian dishes make perfect one-dish party dishes. For one thing, they are relatively expandable for unexpected guests or shrinkable if there are dropouts. Many are even dressy, signature dishes in many parts of Asia and if nothing else, show that the cook is preparing a special meal. A number like *popiah* are so elaborate that they are only prepared for a party. The great thing about most of these recipes is that most parts of the dish are prepared ahead of time, the guests can be left to serve themselves, and you can enjoy the socialising instead of being stuck in the kitchen doing last minute pan-frying. If you have the right equipment to boil the noodles or soup at the table, even boiling noodles or ladling in hot soup can be left to the guests. Not all call for expensive ingredients or if they do, only a small amount is needed. Some such as the wraps are fun meals that get your guests talking about what they are eating.

If the idea of a party with just one dish sounds mingy given the Asian penchant for presenting a groaning board when having guests over, think of the effort you are putting into preparing this one dish. One dish lovingly prepared is worth any number brought in by a caterer. But if you must, the quickest way is to add something that will complement the big-star dish. Pickles that have been prepared way ahead complement many Asian one-dish meals such as pilafs. A vegetable soup, stir-fried vegetables, raita or yoghurt sauce or dip and vegetable sticks will dress up the meal very quickly. There are suggestions for these side dishes, the recipes for which can be found in The Basics (page 9). Many cooks find the day of a party not the day to enjoy their own cooking but it becomes a different story when everyone has left. So it is a plus that not a few of these party dishes make great leftovers.

Popiah  (Straits Chinese Spring Rolls)

Preparation time: 4–5 hours   Serves 5–6

This is the star of Straits Chinese one-dish meals but one not undertaken lightly because it does take time to turn out, especially if you cannot get fresh *popiah* skins and have to make them yourself. Frozen *popiah* skins (a Singapore export worldwide) which once used to be good only for fried spring rolls have improved considerably and will make a decent enough substitute. However, here are recipes for both egg and flour skins, the egg skins being the easier of the two to make. The modified method I have come up with is easy as well although the results may not be as thin as skins made the traditional way. To make flour skins the traditional way takes quite a bit of practice. It calls for holding a slippery ball of damp dough that has to be smeared on a hot pan to form each piece of skin. It is fast if you have acquired the skill for swirling the dough on the pan and lifting the dough up, leaving behind a thin skin. My modified way takes a little longer to do but is much easier. Do the skins and garnishes the day of the party. You could even turn the preparations into a *popiah*-making party with guests pitching in with the work before they tuck in.

FLOUR SKINS (MAKES ABOUT 50 PIECES)

Plain flour	800 g (1³/₄ lb / 4 cups)
Bread flour	300 g (11 oz / 1¹/₂ cups)
Salt	1¹/₂ tsp
Water	800 ml (26 fl oz / 3¹/₄ cups)
Greaseproof paper	as needed, cut into 23-cm (9-in) squares

1. In a mixing bowl, stir together flours, salt and water until all lumps are gone. If dough is very dry, add 2–3 Tbsp more water to get a very soft dough. Cover with plastic wrap and rest for a couple of hours.

2. If you have a cake mixer, use it to beat the dough until it is elastic and shiny but still very soft and damp. The beating or slamming develops the gluten which is what makes the dough feel "ropey". The gluten makes it possible to swing the dough on and off the pan when making *popiah* skin the traditional way. (To do skins the traditional way, reduce the amount of water added to get a stiffer dough.)

3. Have ready a silicon spatula with a rounded bottom, a large piece of greaseproof paper for wrapping the skins, and a 30-cm (12-in) non-stick frying pan.

4. Heat pan to low-medium hot. The pan should be just hot enough to catch the dough but not so hot that the skin cooks too quickly. You should be able to touch the sides of the pan briefly without discomfort.

5. To form the skin, scoop up about a tablespoonful of dough with the spatula and drop it on the hot pan. Quickly spread dough to form a thin skin about 20-cm (8-in) wide. Smooth and spread out raised lumps and mend any holes or too-thin spots with more smears of dough. Once there are no more white spots, the skin looks translucent, and the edges start to curl up, lift the skin off the pan by the edges onto the greaseproof paper. It should take about 15–20 seconds to cook depending on how thin the skin is. Interleave each piece of skin with a square of greaseproof paper to prevent them from sticking together or tearing when you pull them apart. Repeat until dough is used up.

6. Wrap skins in non-stick greaseproof paper and store in a resealable plastic bag until needed.

7. Unused skins may be frozen for another day or use to make fried spring rolls.

EGG SKINS (MAKES ABOUT 50 PIECES)

Eggs	12
Plain flour	750 g (1 lb 11 oz)
Water	2.25 litres (72 fl oz / 9 cups)
Salt	1/2 tsp

1. Using a wire whisk, beat eggs, flour and water together to get a thin, smooth batter. The batter must be stirred up every time before you ladle a spoonful into the pan.

2. Heat a 20-cm (8-in) non-stick pan over medium-low heat. The pan should be hot enough for the batter to start changing colour a few seconds after the batter is in the pan, but not so hot that it sizzles and forms bubbles. Quickly swirl the batter to coat the bottom of the pan.

3. Watch for the bubble that builds up under the skin and as the top of the skin begins to be dry to the touch. When the surface of the skin is no longer tacky, it is done. Lift onto a plate. It should take 15–20 seconds.

4. Repeat until the batter is used up.

5. Keep skins in a plastic box until ready to use.

FILLING 1

Bamboo shoots	1 kg (2 lb 3 oz), finely shredded
Cooking oil	4 Tbsp
Chopped garlic	1 Tbsp
Fermented soy beans (*taucheo*)	2 Tbsp, rinsed and mashed
Light soy sauce	2 Tbsp
Dark soy sauce	2 tsp
Salt	1 1/2 tsp
Pork stock (page 21)	1.5 litres (48 fl oz / 6 cups)

1. If using fresh bamboo shoots, boil in several changes of water for an hour or so. Skip this step if using canned bamboo shoots. Shred bamboo shoots finely by hand.

2. Heat oil in a pot and fry garlic until fragrant before adding fermented soy beans. Fry for a minute, then add bamboo shoots, soy sauces, salt and water and bring to the boil. Turn down heat and simmer for an hour or so, adding more liquid if necessary. Note that the bamboo shoots will remain al dente despite the long boiling but it will become more flavourful.

FILLING 2

Yam bean	800 g (1³/₄ lb), finely shredded
Carrots	200 g (7 oz), peeled and finely shredded
Cooking oil	4 Tbsp
Chopped garlic	1 Tbsp
Dried prawns	1 Tbsp, rinsed and chopped
Fermented soy beans (*taucheo*)	1 Tbsp, rinsed and mashed
Light soy sauce	2 Tbsp
Dark soy sauce	2 tsp
Salt	1¹/₂ tsp
Pork stock (page 21)	1.5 litres (48 fl oz / 6 cups)

1. Shred yam bean and carrots by hand.
2. Fry garlic and dried prawns, until fragrant, then add fermented soy beans, followed by yam bean, sauces and stock. The carrots go in towards the end as shredded carrots soften fairly quickly.

GARNISH

Lettuce (soft leaf variety)	1 large bunch
Garlic	2 heads, peeled and finely pounded
Cooked dried red chilli paste (page 14)	¹/₂ cup
Sweet flour sauce (available in Chinese stores)	as needed
Peeled boiled prawns/crabmeat	200 g (7 oz), deveined and halved
Chinese sausages	2, grilled and thinly sliced
Bean sprouts	100 g (3¹/₂ oz), blanched
Fried garlic (page 11)	1 cup
Cucumber	100 g (3¹/₂ oz), shredded
Hard-boiled eggs	4, peeled and chopped
Chopped coriander leaves	1 cup

1. To make *popiah*, spread a piece of skin on a plate. Put a lettuce leaf in the middle and spread garlic, cooked chilli paste and sweet flour sauce to taste on the leaf. Add a couple of tablespoons of filling and garnish with the prawns/crabmeat, Chinese sausages, bean sprouts, fried garlic, shredded cucumber, egg and coriander leaves before rolling up.

Filipino Seafood Wraps

Preparation time: 1–2 hours   Serves 5–6

This is a special treat that can be made with just boiled prawns, crabmeat, scallops or a combination of seafood including squid and even lobster. Freshly-shelled crabmeat works best but will take more time than using canned or frozen crabmeat. Dress the salad with plain mayonnaise to speed things up or with a Filipino dressing of fresh coconut cream and lime juice. It does not matter if the salad is a trifle wet because of the coconut cream dressing. The rice in the wrap will absorb the dressing.

Tomatoes	300 g (11 oz)
Celery	150 g (5$^1/_3$ oz), chopped
Onion	25 g (1 oz), peeled and chopped
Crabmeat	300 g (11 oz)
Peeled boiled prawns	300 g (11 oz), chopped
Boiled scallops	200 g (7 oz), chopped
Fried garlic and garlic oil (page 11)	1$^1/_2$ Tbsp
Cooked rice	3 cups (from 225 g / 8 oz / 1$^1/_2$ rice cooker cups rice)
Lettuce	500 g (1 lb 1$^1/_2$ oz)

FILIPINO DRESSING

Mayonnaise/ fresh coconut cream	4 Tbsp
Salt	$^1/_2$ tsp
Lime juice/white vinegar	1 Tbsp

1. Prepare dressing first. Mix mayonnaise/coconut cream with salt and lime juice/white vinegar to taste. Set aside.
2. Using a sharp paring knife, skin tomatoes. Halve, then scoop out juicy seeds. Chop tomatoes to the preferred texture.
3. Chop celery and onion to about the same size as tomatoes.
4. Put tomatoes, celery, onion and seafood in a large mixing bowl and dress with either Filipino dressing or plain mayonnaise. Adjust seasoning to taste.
5. Serve salad in a large bowl with a serving spoon or in individual bowls.
6. To make a wrap, spoon seafood salad and some rice on a lettuce leaf and roll up.

Indo-Chinese Noodle Rolls

Preparation time: 2 hours   Serves 5–6

This dish can be tailored to personal taste. While the recipe suggests flaked fish, you can substitute with ready-grilled shredded chicken or thinly sliced roast pork. You can also substitute fresh for pickled vegetables or have a mix of both. Traditional wrappers are the dark green ovoid leaves of *Piper sarmentosum roxb* that grows wild in South East Asia. However, you can substitute with lettuce leaves. Fresh coarse rice vermicelli can also be substituted with rice.

Boneless fish fillet	500 g (1 lb 1$\frac{1}{2}$ oz)
Fish sauce	4 Tbsp
Coriander leaves	1 bunch, finely chopped
Spring onion	1, finely chopped
Tamarind paste	50 g (1$\frac{2}{3}$ oz)
Water	125 ml (4 fl oz / $\frac{1}{2}$ cup)
Chicken/pork/beef stock (pages 20–21)	250 ml (8 fl oz / 1 cup)
Cooking oil	1 Tbsp
Fresh coarse rice vermicelli	400 g (14$\frac{1}{3}$ oz) or 250 g (9 oz / 1$\frac{1}{4}$ cups) rice
Blanched green beans/ long beans/cabbage	300 g (11 oz), finely shredded
Pickled vegetables (page 25)	2 cups, finely shredded
Pickled young ginger (page 25)	1 Tbsp
Red chillies	2, seeded and finely chopped
Fried garlic (page 11)	1 Tbsp
Pointed pepper leaves (*daun kadok*) or lettuce leaves	400 g (14$\frac{1}{3}$ oz)
Assorted fresh herbs (*krachai*, *krachai* leaves, sawtooth herb, turmeric leaves, basil, mint, young galangal)	6 cups, chopped and finely shredded

1. Prepare fish first. Rub fish with 1 Tbsp fish sauce and stand for 15 minutes. Grill or fry fish until cooked. Flake fish and toss with some coriander leaves and spring onion and arrange on a large serving plate.

2. To cook noodles or rice, combine tamarind paste and water, then strain away solids. Mix tamarind juice with stock, 3 Tbsp fish sauce and oil in a pot.

3. If cooking noodles, bring this mixture to the boil and add noodles. Keep it on the boil until noodles are on the soft side. Drain noodles, then snip into short pieces. Arrange noodles with fish on the serving plate.

4. If cooking rice, increase stock, water and tamarind juice to 625 ml (20 fl oz / 2$\frac{1}{2}$ cups). Add 1 Tbsp oil and use to cook rice using your preferred method. Fluff up cooked rice and arrange on the platter with fish.

5. Mix together blanched and pickled vegetables, ginger, chillies and fried garlic. Add fish sauce or salt to taste if needed. Arrange on platter with fish. Serve with vinegar-chilli dip (page 16) made with fish sauce rather than light soy sauce.

6. To make a roll, fill a pointed pepper leaf or lettuce leaf with some noodles or rice, fish, vegetables and herbs. Roll up and dip into vinegar-chilli dip.

Laotian Pork Salad

Preparation time: 1 hour   Serves 5–6

In the non-Muslim parts of Asia, pork is a favourite meat and as elsewhere in South East Asia, the favoured cut is belly pork with its layers of lean and fat. To make this a one-dish meal, wrap this salad with cooked rice in lettuce or pointed pepper leaves.

Tamarind paste	50 g (1²/₃ oz)
Water	500 ml (16 fl oz / 2 cups)
Belly pork	300 g (11 oz)
Fish sauce	2 Tbsp
Indo-Chinese dressing (page 15)	4 Tbsp
Cooked short-grain rice	3 cups (from 225 g / 8 oz / 1¹/₂ rice cooker cups rice)
Pointed pepper leaves (*daun kadok*)/lettuce leaves	as needed

VEGETABLES AND HERBS

Pickled garlic (page 25)	10 cloves, peeled and thinly sliced
Cabbage	200 g (7 oz / 1 cup), finely shredded
Red chillies	3, seeded and chopped
Cucumber	200 g (7 oz / 1 cup), shredded
Tomato	200 g (7 oz / 1 cup), seeded and cut into small wedges
Kaffir lime leaves	3, finely shredded
Krachai leaves	3, finely shredded
Mint	¹/₄ cup
Spring onions	3, chopped
Coriander leaves	1 small bunch, chopped

1. Mix tamarind paste with 500 ml (16 fl oz / 2 cups) water and strain away solids. Add belly pork and fish sauce into tamarind water in a pot and bring to the boil. Turn down heat and simmer until pork is cooked, turning pork over half-way to cook the other side. Cool and slice pork thinly into small strips.

2. Put pork, vegetables and herbs into a mixing bowl and stir in Indo-Chinese dressing.

3. Serve with cooked short-grain rice and leaves for wrapping pork salad.

Vietnamese Salad Rolls

Preparation time: 2 hours   Serves 5–6

Rice paper becomes tender when softened in water, unlike spring roll skin which remains chewy. Substitute with lettuce leaves if dried rice paper is not available. These spring rolls are usually served as appetisers but they make an excellent main dish if you eat enough of them. What takes time to cook is the belly pork. Substitute with chicken if preferred.

Tamarind paste	25 g (1 oz)
Water	1 litre (32 fl oz / 4 cups)
Fish sauce	4 Tbsp
Belly pork	400 g (14$\frac{1}{3}$ oz)
Prawns	1 kg (2 lb 3 oz), deveined, boiled, peeled and sliced in half
Cucumber	750 g (1 lb 11 oz), cored and sliced
Carrot	250 g (9 oz), peeled and finely shredded
Salt	1 tsp
Rice paper	
Bowls of cold water	
Damp clean hand towels	1 per person
Assorted fresh herbs, at least three kinds (mint, sawtooth herb, laksa leaves, basil, coriander leaves, spring onion)	8 cups

VIETNAMESE PEANUT DIP

Cooking oil	3 Tbsp
Garlic	3 cloves, peeled and mashed
Chinese hot bean sauce	3 Tbsp
Water	250 ml (8 fl oz / 1 cup)
Sugar	75 g (2$\frac{2}{3}$ oz / $\frac{1}{3}$ cup)
Fish sauce	125 ml (4 fl oz / $\frac{1}{2}$ cup)
Chinese plum sauce	3 Tbsp
Large lime juice	3 Tbsp
Toasted and ground peanuts	100 g (3$\frac{1}{2}$ oz / $\frac{1}{2}$ cup)

1. Prepare dip. Heat oil in a saucepan and sauté garlic until fragrant. Add hot bean sauce and fry for another minute. Add remaining ingredients except peanuts and bring to the boil. Lower heat, add peanuts and adjust seasoning to taste. Cool and bottle until needed. When bottled, dip will thicken because of the peanuts. Dilute with some water if so.

2. Prepare belly pork. In a saucepan, mix tamarind paste with 1 litre (32 fl oz / 4 cups) water. Strain and discard the solids. Add pork and fish sauce. Bring to the boil, lower heat and simmer until pork is tender. Cool and slice thinly. Arrange on a large platter and cover to prevent crusting.

3. Arrange boiled prawns with pork.

4. Brine cucumber with 1 tsp salt, stand for 30 minutes, then squeeze out the water. Arrange salted cucumber, shredded carrot with pork and prawns.

5. Have assorted herbs on the same platter or in separate bowls.

6. Give each guest a bowl of cold water and a small damp hand towel on a plate.

7. To make a roll, first dip a sheet of rice paper in the bowl of cold water and spread it out on the damp hand towel. Do not soak the rice paper or it will disintegrate. Properly thin rice paper is fragile if too wet. Top softened rice paper with pork, prawn, cucumber, carrot and herbs of choice. Roll up and enjoy with dip.

Banh Chung (Vietnamese Rice Dumplings)

Preparation time: 3 hours   Makes 4–5 bundles, serving 5–6

The Vietnamese make these rice dumplings to celebrate Tet, the Vietnamese Lunar New Year. Tet celebrations mean several days of enjoyment and feasting and these dumplings are perfect because they are made ahead and once cooked, can be kept over several days, and be eaten on their own, with leaf wrappings and a Vietnamese style salad or with other dishes. The dumplings can be made from scratch with raw rice, but I always find wrapping steamed rice easier. Mung dhal is skinned split mung beans which also comes split with the green skins still on or whole with the green skins. The beans with skin have more texture while mung dhal dissolves into the rice and gives the glutinous rice more mouth-feel.

White glutinous rice	450 g (1 lb / 2$^1/_4$ cups / 3 rice cooker cups), soaked overnight
Salt	1 tsp
Water	375 ml (12 fl oz / 1$^1/_2$ cups)
Indo-Chinese dressing (page 15)	as needed
Pointed pepper leaves (*daun kadok*)/lettuce leaves	

FILLING

Mung dhal/mung beans	200 g (7 oz / 1 cup), soaked 1 hour
Cooking oil	2 Tbsp
Shallots	25 g (1 oz), peeled and chopped
Fish sauce	2 Tbsp
Ground black pepper	1 tsp
Sugar	2 tsp
Salt	$^1/_2$ tsp
Belly pork/pork shoulder	300 g (11 oz), cut into small strips
Water	125 ml (4 fl oz / $^1/_2$ cup)

FOR WRAPPING

Banana leaves	6–10, each 50 x 30-cm (19$^1/_2$ x 12-in)
Straw twine or raffia string	
Cooking oil	

1. Cook rice with salt and water in a rice cooker. Leave rice in covered pot to cool, then divide into 4 or 5 equal portions.

2. Boil mung dhal/mung beans with plenty of water until tender but still whole or cook in a slow cooker overnight. Drain and divide into 4 or 5 equal portions.

3. To make meat filling, heat oil in a wok and fry shallots until fragrant and brown. Stir in all other ingredients for filling and simmer over low heat until pork is tender and filling only slightly moist. About 15 minutes should do it although it does depend on the size of the strips of meat and how tender it is. Divide filling into 4 or 5 equal portions.

4. Blanch banana leaves in hot water or singe over a gas burner or hot plate. If leaves have been blanched, wipe dry and clean with a wad of dry paper towels. If leaves have been singed, wipe clean with a wad of damp paper towels.

5. To wrap dumplings, have on hand a bowl of cold water and a small bowl of oil for greasing leaves.

6. Lay a banana leaf on a flat surface. Brush liberally with oil. Using wet hands, flatten a portion of rice to a rectangle about 25 x 15 cm (10 x 6 in). Spread one portion of dhal/beans on rice, topped with a portion of meat filling in the centre.

7. Fold long sides of banana leaf over filling, then fold short ends under the parcel. Secure parcel with straw twine or raffia string.

8. Steam wrapped dumplings for 30 minutes.

9. To serve rice dumplings, unwrap, then cut each roll into 6–8 pieces. The dumplings can be served cold or warm, on its own or with a salad or pickles. It can also be served with pepper leaf wraps and a choice of fresh herbs (laksa leaves, mint leaves, coriander leaves or spring onion). Serve with Indo-Chinese dressing as the condiment. Dilute with water, fish and lime juice if preferred.

TIP

If the banana leaves are not large enough, overlap pieces of banana leaf to make up the required size.

Bulgogi Salad Platter

Preparation time: 1 hour   Serves 5–6

A *bulgogi* salad platter is a very tasty way of serving this quintessential Korean barbecue that is usually grilled at the table. However, this one-dish party fare can be simplified by cooking the *bulgogi* in the kitchen and arranging it all on a platter for guests to help themselves. The easy availability of kimchi simplifies this dish. You can now find the standard Tientsin cabbage kimchi or even radish kimchi. Substitute kimchi with pickled vegetables (page 25) if not available. If you can get kimchi, do not discard the pickling juice in the bottle of kimchi. It is excellent flavouring for a quick soup (page 23).

Romaine lettuce	1 kg (2 lb 3 oz)
Radish kimchi	200 g (7 oz)
Tientsin cabbage kimchi	300 g (11 oz)
Garlic	2 heads, peeled
Cooked short-grain rice	3 cups (from 225 g / 8 oz / 1¹/₂ rice cooker cups rice)
Vegetable oil	1 Tbsp
BULGOGI	
Ginger	5-cm (2-in) knob, peeled and pounded
Beef/chicken	500 g (1 lb 1¹/₂ oz), thinly sliced
Garlic	4 cloves, peeled and pounded
Sesame oil	2 Tbsp
Dark soy sauce	1 tsp
Salt	1 tsp
Sugar	3 Tbsp
Spring onions	3, chopped

1. Season bulgogi first. It can be done overnight. Squeeze juice from pounded ginger on beef/chicken and discard pulp. Add rest of seasoning and mix well with meat. Cover and stand for 1 hour or overnight in the fridge.

2. Clean lettuce and spin or shake dry. Keep leaves whole. Arrange on a large serving platter.

3. Slice radish and cabbage kimchi into thin strips. If preferred, slice garlic thinly, chop, or keep as whole cloves. Arrange on serving platter.

4. Heat oil in a frying pan until hot. Add marinated meat and stir-fry until meat is cooked or about 2 minutes depending on size of the strips. Beef takes less time than chicken. Arrange bulgogi on the serving platter with the other ingredients.

5. Give each diner a small bowl of rice and a pair of chopsticks. Make a wrap with the lettuce leaf and the other ingredients, including rice. Keep parcel small enough to eat up in three bites.

Penang Joo Hoo Char (Lettuce Wraps with Yam Bean and Dried Squid)

Preparation time: 1 hour   Serves 5–6

This dish tastes better if made several hours ahead of time or even a day ahead. Leftovers freeze well so long as the yam bean, also known as bangkuang or jicama is not overcooked. Thinly sliced dried squid ready for cooking this dish can now be found in Singapore and Malaysian market stalls and Asian stores. If not, look for whole dried squid and slice thinly with a sharp knife. If you find the flavour too intense, reduce the amount of dried squid.

Dried squid	50 g (1^2/$_3$ oz)
Cooking oil	3 Tbsp
Chopped garlic	1 Tbsp
Yam bean	600 g (1 lb 5^1/$_3$ oz), peeled, rinsed and finely shredded
Pork/chicken/prawn stock (pages 20–21)	500 ml (16 fl oz / 2 cups)
Light soy sauce	1^1/$_2$ Tbsp
Dark soy sauce	a few drops
Salt	^{1}/$_2$ tsp
Lettuce leaves	500 g (1 lb 1^1/$_2$ oz)

1. If you are using whole dried squid, rinse well. Discard the plastic-like piece in the middle and using a sharp knife, slice dried squid into very thin, short strips. Skip this step if using ready-sliced dried squid.

2. Heat oil in a wok and sauté garlic until fragrant.

3. Add yam bean, squid, stock, soy sauces and salt and bring to the boil. Simmer for 15 minutes or until yam bean is the preferred texture. Keep yam bean fairly moist to make reheating easier.

4. To serve, spoon some of the warm filling onto a lettuce leaf and roll up.

Burmese Rice Salad Wraps

Preparation time: 1 hour   Serves 5–6

This rice salad is the Burmese version of Malay *nasi ulam* but with a pointed pepper leaf wrapping. Substitute with lettuce leaves if desired. It makes a great party dish because of its potential for expansion.

Cooked rice	4 cups (from 300 g / 11 oz / 2 rice cooker cups rice)
Salt	$^1/_2$ tsp
Onion	50 g ($1^2/_3$ oz), peeled and thinly sliced
Cucumber	200 g (7 oz), shredded
Fried shallots (page 11)	1 Tbsp
Fried garlic (page 11)	1 Tbsp
Spring onions	3, large, chopped
Coriander leaves	1 large bunch, chopped
Dhal/rice/fish/prawn/vegetable crackers/potato chips	as needed
Pointed pepper leaves (*daun kadok*) or lettuce leaves	as needed

FISH DRESSING

Salt	1 tsp
Ground turmeric	1 tsp
Boneless fish fillet	400 g ($14^1/_3$ oz)
Cooking oil	4 Tbsp
Chopped tomatoes	$^1/_2$ cup
Chopped onion	$^1/_2$ cup
Ginger	4 slices, finely shredded
Chilli powder	1 tsp
Lime juice	$^1/_2$ Tbsp

1. Prepare fish dressing first. Mix salt and turmeric together and rub into fish.

2. Heat oil in a wok and fry fish until cooked. Cool fish and flake it, discarding any bones.

3. In the same hot oil used for frying fish, fry tomatoes, onion, ginger and chilli powder until oil starts to surface. Add flaked fish and lime juice and mix well.

4. In a mixing bowl, stir together three-quarters of the fish dressing with cooked rice, salt, onion, cucumber, fried shallots and garlic. Add spring onions and coriander leaves.

5. Dish dressed rice out on a serving plate and garnish with remaining fish dressing and crushed crackers or potato chips.

6. To serve, make salad into rolls using a pointed pepper leaf or lettuce leaf.

Gado-Gado (Indonesian Mixed Vegetable Platter)

Preparation time: 2 hours   Serves 5–6

The preparation time required depends on whether the essential dressing or sauce comes in a packet or you are making it from scratch. (The sauce freezes well.) Practically everything else is just a matter of trimming and blanching, boiling or light frying. Look for these peanut sauce concentrates common to a number of Indonesian-Malay dishes in Asian stores. They may be labelled as "*pecel*" or "*jaganan*" but not *gado-gado,* as this is the name of the dish. All that is needed is to add water/tamarind juice, boil it up and adjust the seasoning to taste. As these packaged sauces tend to be super-spicy, you might want to reduce the heat by adding more ground peanuts and adjust the seasoning accordingly.

Cabbage	200 g (7 oz), coarsely shredded
Bean sprouts	200 g (7 oz), tails removed
Long beans/French beans	100 g (3$\frac{1}{2}$ oz), cut into finger lengths
Cucumber	200 g (7 oz), sliced or cut into small chunks
Potatoes	400 g (14$\frac{1}{3}$ oz), boiled, peeled and cubed
Hard-boiled eggs	6, peeled and halved
Cooking oil for frying	
Firm bean curd	300 g (11 oz)
Tempeh	100 g (3$\frac{1}{2}$ oz)
Fried prawn/vegetable crackers	a few large pieces

GADO-GADO SAUCE

Shallots	200 g (7 oz), peeled
Garlic	100 g (3$\frac{1}{2}$ oz), peeled
Dried prawn paste (*belacan*)	1 tsp
Cooked dried red chilli paste (page 14)	50 g (1$\frac{2}{3}$ oz / $\frac{1}{4}$ cup)
Cooking oil	5 Tbsp
Tamarind paste	75 g (2$\frac{2}{3}$ oz) or 3 Tbsp white vinegar
Water	1 litre (32 fl oz / 4 cups)
Salt	1$\frac{1}{2}$ tsp
Sugar	75 g (2$\frac{2}{3}$ oz / $\frac{1}{3}$ cup)
Toasted and ground peanuts (page 10)	300 g (11 oz / 1$\frac{1}{2}$ cups)
Fried shallots (page 11)	2 Tbsp

1. To make *gado-gado* sauce, blend together shallots, garlic, dried prawn paste and cooked dried red chilli paste in a food processor until fine. Add a bit of water if necessary.

2. Heat oil in a large saucepan and fry ground ingredients until oil surfaces.

3. If using tamarind paste, mix it with the water and strain away solids. Pour tamarind juice or water and vinegar into the saucepan. Add salt, sugar and peanuts and bring to the boil. Turn down heat and simmer for another 5 minutes. Adjust seasoning to taste.

4. Stir in fried shallots. Set aside while preparing salad ingredients.

5. Bring a pot of water to the boil and blanch cabbage, then bean sprouts for 10 seconds each. Return water to the boil and cook long beans/French beans for 3 minutes. Drain vegetables well and arrange on a large platter.

6. On the same platter with the boiled vegetables, arrange cucumber, potatoes and hard-boiled eggs.

7. Heat some oil in a frying pan and brown bean curd and tempeh on both sides. Cut into bite-size pieces. Arrange with vegetables.

8. To serve, put a selection of vegetables, bean curd, tempeh and egg in a deep dish. Pour some sauce over the salad and garnish with a few pieces of prawn or

Prawn Mee Soup, Penang-style

Preparation time: 2 hours   Serves 5–6

The easy way to prepare this dish is to always have some prawn and pork stock in the freezer. Penang-style prawn *mee* is spicier than Singapore-style prawn *mee* because of the chilli paste added to the soup. Like Singapore-style prawn *mee*, yellow Hokkien *mee* can be combined or substituted with thin rice vermicelli.

Prawn stock (page 20)	500 ml (16 fl oz / 2 cups)
Prawns	500 g (1 lb 1$\frac{1}{2}$ oz)
Water convolvulus	500 g (1 lb 1$\frac{1}{2}$ oz)
Bean sprouts	250 g (9 oz)
Hokkien *mee*	600 g (1 lb 5 oz) or substitute half with rice vermicelli
Cooked dried red chilli paste (page 14)	to taste

SOUP

Water	2 litres (64 fl oz / 8 cups)
Pork ribs with meat	1 kg (2 lb 3 oz)
Pig's tail	1, chop into short lengths
Salt	1$\frac{1}{2}$ tsp
Cooked dried red chilli paste (page 14)	1 Tbsp
Fried shallots (page 11)	1 Tbsp
Dried prawn paste (*belacan*)	1 tsp

GARNISH

Fried shallots (page 11)	$\frac{1}{2}$ cup

1. Start by preparing the soup first. Put the water, pork ribs and pig's tail into a stock pot and bring to the boil. Skim off the scum that rises to the top. Add the rest of the ingredients and simmer over low heat until meat is tender. This should take about 1$\frac{1}{2}$ hours.

2. While soup is simmering, bring prawn stock to the boil in another pot. Add prawns and when prawns turn pink, remove them. Cool, then peel, leaving tails on. Return prawn shells and heads to prawn stock and simmer for 10 minutes. Discard shells and heads.

3. Add prawn stock to soup when soup is done and return to the boil. Adjust seasoning to taste.

4. Prepare water convolvulus by rinsing clean and cutting into short lengths. If the stems are thick, split in half.

5. To serve noodles, bring a pot of water to the boil. Blanch bean sprouts for 10 seconds. Scoop out and divide into serving bowls.

6. Return water to the boil and blanch water convolvulus for 10 seconds. Scoop out and divide into the serving bowls.

7. Return water to the boil and blanch Hokkien *mee* until noodles are tender but al dente. If combining *mee* with rice vermicelli, boil the two types of noodles separately. Divide and place into the serving bowls.

8. Ladle hot soup over noodles, then top with pieces of meat, pig's tail and some prawns. Garnish with fried shallots.

9. Serve hot with cooked dried red chilli paste and an empty dish for the bones.

Sukiyaki Udon

Preparation time: 1 hour   Serves 5–6

Sukiyaki is a Japanese one-pot meal traditionally cooked at the table. It can be simplified by cooking in the kitchen and serving in individual bowls or mixed together into one large communal pan and dished out into individual serving bowls. Preparing this dish is speeded up if you can buy sukiyaki beef from the supermarket. This is very thinly sliced beef and if it is available, you will also be given a piece of suet for rubbing on the pan to cook the beef. Do your own thin slices of beef if sukiyaki beef is not available. Udon can be substituted with glass noodles or sweet potato noodles if preferred.

Sukiyaki beef	500 g (1 lb 1^1/$_2$ oz)
Sake	2 Tbsp
Dried udon	300 g (11 oz)
Cooking oil	1 Tbsp
Firm bean curd	100 g (3^1/$_2$ oz)
Leeks	4 stalks, cut into 3-cm (1-in) lengths
Fresh shiitake mushrooms	8 pieces, wiped clean, sliced thickly or quartered
Chrysanthemum leaves	500 g (1 lb 1^1/$_2$ oz), cut into 3-cm (1-in) lengths
Shichimi togarashi (page 16)	
Pickled vegetables (page 25)	

SAUCE

Light soy sauce	125 ml (4 fl oz / ^{1}/$_2$ cup)
Dark soy sauce	1 Tbsp
Mirin	4 Tbsp
Water	250 ml (8 fl oz / 1 cup)

1. If thinly sliced sukiyaki beef is not available, do your own. Freeze the piece of beef until firm but not rock-hard. Using a sharp knife, slice beef across the grain as thinly as you can. Marinate beef in sake for 15 minutes.

2. Combine sauce ingredients in a small pot and simmer for 1 minute to dissolve the sugar. Set aside.

3. Bring a large pot of salted water to the boil and cook udon until tender but still al dente. Drain well and divide into serving bowls. Alternatively, set aside the boiled noodles until ready to stir noodles with the other cooked ingredients in the pan before dishing out.

4. Heat oil in a frying pan and brown both sides of bean curd. Cut into thick slices.

5. Remove all but 1 tsp oil from pan and add enough sauce to form a 0.5-cm (^{1}/$_4$-in) layer in the pan and bring it to the boil. Spread pieces of beef flat in the sauce and cook meat for 10 seconds. Add more sauce as it dries out. Set aside cooked beef.

6. Put remainder of sauce into the pan and bring to the boil. Add bean curd, leeks and mushrooms and simmer for 1 minute or until leeks are limp. Stir in the chrysanthemum leaves last.

7. All the cooked ingredients can be returned to the pan and stirred together with guests helping themselves from the communal pan or divided into individual serving bowls. Divide and place cooked vegetables into the bowls of udon and top with slices of beef and sauce. Serve immediately with *shichimi togarashi* and pickled vegetables.

TIP
If mirin is not available, substitute with sake or Chinese rice wine and add sugar to taste.

Ch'aebansomyon (Wheat Noodles in Dipping Sauce, Korean-style)

Preparation time: 1 hour   Serves 5–6

Serve this Korean-style cold noodles on slatted bamboo mats placed in a bowl to drain the noodles. The dipping sauce can be made overnight or use bottled Japanese soup concentrate which can be found in Japanese supermarkets. Dilute it with cold water. Korean *somyon* and Japanese *somen*, both made from wheat, can be substituted with Chinese fine wheat vermicelli (*mee sua*). However, Chinese vermicelli tends to be a little more salty than *somyon* or *somen*.

Cucumber	100 g (3^1/$_2$ oz)
Salt	^{1}/$_2$ tsp
Cooking oil for frying	
Eggs	2, beaten
Crabsticks	6 pieces, shredded
Spring onions	3, shredded
Fresh shiitake mushrooms	4, thinly sliced
Chrysanthemum leaves	1 bunch
Korean dried *somyon*/ Japanese *somen*	400 g (14^1/$_3$ oz)
Nori strips	a handful
Korean sesame salt (page 17) or *shichimi togarashi* (page 16)	

DIPPING SAUCE

Dried anchovies/ dried mushrooms	5 pieces/5 small pieces
Water	750 ml (24 fl oz / 3 cups)
Konbu	6-cm (2.5-in) piece
Sugar	^{1}/$_2$ Tbsp
Shoju (Korean rice wine)/sake	1 Tbsp
Korean light soy sauce	2 Tbsp
Ground black pepper	a large pinch

1. Start by preparing the dipping sauce. If using anchovies, remove stomachs and heads from the fish and rinse briefly. If using dried mushrooms, slice mushrooms thinly.

2. Combine water, konbu and anchovies/mushrooms in a saucepan and bring to the boil. Turn down heat and simmer for 10 minutes. Strain stock and discard solids.

3. Stir sugar into hot stock. Cool stock, then stir in *shoju*, light soy sauce and pepper. Chill in the fridge for at least an hour or overnight.

4. Cut cucumber into thin strips and rub 1/2 tsp salt into them. Stand for 10 minutes, then squeeze out the water. Arrange cucumber on one side of bamboo trays.

5. Heat some oil in a frying pan and make 4–5 paper-thin omelettes out of beaten eggs. Slice into thin strips and arrange on one side of bamboo trays.

6. Arrange shredded crabsticks and shredded spring onions next to egg and cucumber strips on trays.

7. Bring a large pot of water to the boil and blanch mushrooms for 5 seconds. Scoop out, drain well and arrange on trays.

8. Return water to the boil and blanch chrysanthemum leaves for 5 seconds. Scoop out and squeeze out excess water by pressing leaves between the scoop and a large spoon. Arrange on trays.

9. Return water to the boil and blanch noodles until tender but al dente. Scoop out and drop into a cold water bath. Drain noodles well. Divide and place noodles on bamboo trays, twirling noodles into a heap in the centre of trays. Top with a few strands of nori.

10. Serve with a small bowl of cold dipping sauce, Korean sesame salt or *shichimi togarashi.*

Penang Laksa (Rice Noodles in Fish Soup, Penang-style)

Preparation time: 2 hours   Serves 5–6

This is definitely a festive dish, something that you would do for a gathering or as a family social. While relatively simple, the number of ingredients do add up. Although the fish traditionally used for Penang laksa is wolf-herring also called *dorab* or *ikan parang (Fam. Chirocentridae Chirocentrus dorab (Foskal)*, this fish is no longer easily available. Substitute with any soft-fleshed fish such as mackerel that flakes easily including canned sardines in tomato sauce. (Discard the tomato sauce.) Laksa leaf is also known as *daun kesom* in Malay or Vietnamese mint in Indo-China.

Torch ginger bud	1 stalk, stem discarded, bud halved
Fresh medium-coarse rice vermicelli	600 g (1 lb 5 oz)
Laksa leaves	1 large bunch
Salt	2 tsp

GRAVY

Tamarind paste	100 g (3$\frac{1}{2}$ oz)
Water	1.5 litres (48 fl oz / 6 cups)
Fish	1 kg (2 lb 3 oz)
Sour fruit slices (*asam gelugor*)	4–6 large pieces

SPICE PASTE

Shallots	200 g (7 oz), peeled
Dried prawn paste (*belacan*)	1 tsp
Red chillies	150 g (5$\frac{1}{3}$ oz), seeded
Water	2 Tbsp

GARNISH

Salt	$\frac{1}{2}$ tsp
Onion	100 g (3$\frac{1}{2}$ oz), peeled and thinly sliced
Black prawn paste (*haeko*)	3 Tbsp
Hot water	4 Tbsp
Cucumber	250 g (9 oz), shredded
Lettuce	2 bunches, shredded
Mint leaves	2 cups
Torch ginger bud	1 stalk, finely shredded
Fresh pineapple	1, coarsely shredded
Red chillies	6, seeded and finely chopped
Lime halves	

1. Prepare spice paste first. Blend all ingredients together in a food processor.

2. Prepare gravy. Mix tamarind paste with water and strain juice into a large pot. Discard solids. Add fish and sour fruit and bring to the boil. Simmer gently until fish is cooked. Remove fish, cool and flake fish. Set aside. Return fish bones and skin to pot and simmer for another 10 minutes. Strain and discard solids.

3. Put spice paste, ginger bud, laksa leaves and salt into gravy and bring to the boil before adding flaked fish. Stir well and return to the boil

4. Prepare garnish. Mix salt into sliced onion, stand for 5 minutes, then squeeze out juice. Arrange salted onion on a serving platter. Dilute black prawn paste with hot water to an even pouring liquid. Place in a small bowl with a spoon. Arrange rest of garnishes on the platter with onion.

5. To serve, bring a large pot of water to the boil. Blanch noodles until tender but still al dente. Divide and place into serving bowls. Ladle hot gravy over noodles and garnish as desired.

Mohinga (Burmese Laksa/Rice Noodles in Fish Soup)

Preparation time: 2 hours   Serves 5–6

This is suitable as a party dish as the ingredients add up to make quite a large dish. The fish of choice is catfish but if not available, substitute with any fish that flakes easily such as mackerel. *Mohinga* served in Burma is often a gray colour because of the banana stems and unripe bananas that enrich the gravy. Look for these in Asian stores patronised by the Burmese and Indo-Chinese.

Uncooked long-grain rice	50 g (1^2/$_3$ oz / ^{1}/$_4$ cup)
Gram dhal/chickpea flour	200 g (7 oz / 1 cup)
Water	1.5 litres (48 fl oz / 6 cups)
Fish	500 g (1 lb 1^1/$_2$ oz)
Fish sauce	3 Tbsp
Salt	^{1}/$_2$ tsp
Ground turmeric	^{1}/$_4$ tsp
Dried red chillies	25 g (1 oz), seeded
Dried prawn paste (*belacan*)	1 tsp
Lemon grass	1 stalk, bruised
Fresh thin/medium rice vermicelli	600 g (1 lb 5^1/$_3$ oz)

SPICE PASTE

Shallots	100 g (3^1/$_2$ oz), peeled
Garlic	3 cloves, peeled
Galangal	2.5-cm (1-in) knob, peeled
Lemon grass	1 stalk, sliced thinly
Water	2 Tbsp
Cooked dried red chilli paste (page 14)	1^1/$_2$ Tbsp

GRAVY

Peanut oil	4 Tbsp
Shallots	12, peeled
Unripe bananas/plantains	2, peeled, halved and sliced 2-cm (^{3}/$_4$-in) thick
Banana stem	30-cm (12-in) length, peeled and sliced 1-cm (^{1}/$_2$-in) thick
Water	4 Tbsp
Toasted peanuts	2 Tbsp, finely ground

GARNISH

Hard-boiled eggs	4, peeled and quartered
Fried fish cake/crabsticks	150 g (5^1/$_3$ oz), thinly sliced
Chopped coriander leaves	1 cup
Fried garlic (page 11)	
Prawn/fish/vegetable/ split-pea crackers	
Toasted red chilli flakes (page 17)	
Lime halves	
Toasted chickpea flour	

1. Prepare spice paste first. Blend shallots, garlic, galangal and lemon grass with 2 Tbsp water until fine. Add cooked dried red chilli paste last. Set aside.

2. Rinse rice clean and dry on a paper towel. Over low heat, dry-fry rice in a frying pan until brown. Cool, then pound to a powder. Over low heat, dry-fry gram dhal/chickpea flour until it no longer smells raw. If using gram dhal, it needs to be pounded to a powder, like the rice. Combine rice powder and 2 Tbsp gram dhal/chickpea flour with 4 Tbsp water, mix well and set aside. Stir up again before adding to gravy.

3. Make fish stock. Place 1.5 litres (48 fl oz / 6 cups) water, fish, fish sauce, salt, turmeric, dried chillies, prawn paste and lemon grass in a pot. Bring to the boil, then lower heat and simmer until fish is cooked. Remove fish from stock. Cool and flake fish. Set aside. Return fish bones to the pot and simmer for another 10 minutes. Using a wire scoop, remove and discard solids. Put flaked fish into stock.

4. To make gravy, heat oil in a frying pan and add spice paste. Fry until fragrant and oil surfaces. Pour contents of pan into stock and return stock to the boil. Add whole shallots and banana/plantain slices and simmer until plantain and shallots are soft. Add banana stem slices half-way through. Stir up rice powder-gram dhal/chickpea flour mixture and add to boiling gravy, stirring it into the gravy.

5. Just before serving, add ground peanuts to gravy. (If added too early, the peanuts swell up and absorb a lot of liquid.)

6. To serve, boil a large pot of water and blanch vermicelli until tender but al dente. Drain well. Divide and place into serving bowls. Arrange garnishes on a large serving platter. Have hot gravy in a large bowl or the pot for guests to help themselves.

Khanom Jeen Nam Ya (Thai Laksa/Rice Noodles in Fish Gravy)

Preparation time: 2 hours   Serves 5–6

Like Burmese mohinga *and Penang laksa, this Thai laksa also features a fish gravy, assorted herbs and rice noodles.*

SPICE PASTE

Garlic	50 g (1^2/$_3$ oz), peeled and quartered
Shallots	100 g (3^1/$_2$ oz), peeled and coarsely sliced
Lemon grass	2 stalks, finely sliced
Krachai	750 g (1 lb 9^1/$_2$ oz), scraped and finely sliced
Galangal	5 slices
Dried prawn paste (*belacan*)	1^1/$_2$ tsp
Dried red chillies	10, seeded and rinsed
Water	250 ml (8 fl oz / 1 cup)

GRAVY

Cooking oil for frying salted fish	
Dried salted fish	50 g (1^2/$_3$ oz), rinsed and thinly sliced
Water	1.25 litres (40 fl oz / 5 cups)
Mackerel	500 g (1 lb 1^1/$_2$ oz), gutted and scaled
Fresh grated coconut	600 g (1 lb 5 oz)
Fish sauce	4 Tbsp
Salt	^{1}/$_2$ tsp
Fresh coarse rice vermicelli	600 g (1 lb 5^1/$_3$ oz)
Prawns	500 g (1 lb 1^1/$_2$ oz), boiled and peeled
Hard-boiled eggs	4, peeled and sliced
Bean sprouts	150 g (5^1/$_3$ oz), rinsed and blanched
French beans	150 g (5^1/$_3$ oz), tailed, rinsed and blanched
Basil leaves	1 cup, rinsed and coarsely chopped
Sawtooth coriander	1 cup, rinsed and finely chopped
Mint	1 cup, rinsed and finely chopped

1. Make spice paste for gravy first. Put all ingredients into a pot and simmer gently for about 10 minutes until shallots are soft. Using a blender, blend ingredients to a smooth paste. Set aside.

2. Heat some oil in a frying pan and fry salted fish over low heat until crisp. Pound fine and set aside for sprinkling over gravy.

3. Heat 250 ml (8 fl oz / 1 cup) water in a small pot and boil mackerel until cooked. Remove fish. Cool and flake fish. Set aside. Return fish trimmings to pot and simmer for another 10 minutes to get fish stock. Strain and discard solids.

4. Mix grated coconut with 250 ml (8 fl oz / 1 cup) water, then squeeze through a muslin bag or cloth-lined sieve to obtain first coconut milk. Set first coconut milk aside.

5. Add remaining water to grated coconut and extract second milk. Pour into a large saucepan. Add spice paste and fish stock and bring to the boil. Add mashed fish, fish sauce and salt and simmer for 3 minutes.

6. Add first coconut milk, stir well and bring to a near-boil. Do not boil or milk will separate. Adjust seasoning to taste. Just before serving, sprinkle ground salted fish into gravy.

7. Prepare garnishes before boiling noodles. Arrange boiled eggs and prawns on a large serving platter. Put chopped herbs in separate small bowls or with vegetables and prawns.

8. Bring a big pot of water to the boil and blanch bean sprouts and French beans separately for 10 seconds. Drain well and arrange on a large platter.

9. Return water to the boil and cook noodles until tender but still al dente. Drain well. Divide and place into serving bowls.

10. Garnish with blanched vegetables and herbs and ladle hot fish stock over noodles. Top with boiled prawns and hard-boiled egg. Serve hot with cooked dried red chilli paste (page 14) or red chillies with fish sauce (page 15).

Sarawak Kolo Mee (Dry Wheat Noodles, Sarawak-style)

Preparation time: 1½ hours   Serves 5–6

The name for this dish, "*kolo mee*", is probably a corruption of the Cantonese phrase "*kon loh meen*" meaning "dry noodles". This noodle dish from East Malaysia is a relative newcomer to the wide range of noodle dishes in Singapore. Use *mee kia*, *mee pok* or Hong Kong noodles for this dish or substitute with dried egg noodles. Note that the dressing for noodles serves one while remaining ingredients serve more.

Cooking oil	3 Tbsp
Shallots	50 g (1²/₃ oz), finely chopped
Fermented soy beans (*taucheo*)/brown miso	1 Tbsp, finely mashed
Minced pork	300 g (11 oz)
Light soy sauce	1 Tbsp
Dark soy sauce	a few drops for colour
Sugar	½ Tbsp
Mustard greens	400 g (14¹/₃ oz), cut into finger lengths
Fresh egg noodles	600 g (1 lb 5 oz)
Prawns	500 g (1 lb 1½ oz), peeled and deveined, leaving tails intact, boiled
Cooked dried red chilli paste (page 14)	
Chinese-style chicken vegetable soup (page 23)	

DRESSING FOR NOODLES (SERVES 1)

Light soy sauce	1 Tbsp
Shallot oil (page 11)	1 Tbsp

1. Heat oil in a pot and fry shallots until golden brown and fragrant. Stir in fermented soy beans/brown miso and mix well, then add minced pork and fry for 1 minute.

2. Stir in soy sauces and sugar and simmer until meat is cooked.

3. Bring a pot of water to the boil and blanch mustard greens for 10 seconds. Scoop out, drain well and set aside.

4. Return water to the boil and blanch noodles until tender but still al dente. Scoop out and drain well. Divide and place into serving plates with dressing. Stir in dressing.

5. Garnish with mustard greens, prawns and a helping of minced pork. Serve immediately with a condiment of cooked dried red chilli paste and a small bowl of soup.

Soto Mee (Noodles in Indonesian Chicken Soup)

Preparation time: 2 hours   Serves 5–6

This Singapore fusion dish combines Indonesia's famous *soto ayam* (chicken soup) with Hokkien *mee* or thin rice vermicelli. In Indonesia, *soto ayam* is sometimes served with cubes of *ketupat* (rice cake) or glass noodles. Chinese celery and coriander leaves are a must in this dish.

Hokkien *mee*	600 g (1 lb 5¹/₃ oz), or 300 g (11 oz) dried thin rice vermicelli
Bean sprouts	200 g (7 oz)

SPICE PASTE

Ginger	50 g (1²/₃ oz), peeled
Garlic	3 cloves, peeled
Water	3 Tbsp
Ground coriander	4 tsp
Ground cumin	3 tsp
Ground turmeric	2 tsp
Ground white pepper	3 tsp

SOUP

Cooking oil	2 Tbsp
Onion	50 g (1²/₃ oz), peeled and finely sliced
Cinnamon stick	4-cm (1¹/₂-in) length
Cloves	4
Cardamoms	4 pods
Lemon grass	3 stalks, bruised
Chicken drumstick or breast	500 g (1 lb 1¹/₂ oz)
Chicken stock (page 20)	1.25 litres (40 fl oz / 5 cups)
Salt	1¹/₂ tsp

BERGEDEL (POTATO CAKE)

Boiled potatoes	300 g (11 oz), peeled and mashed
Salt	¹/₄ tsp
Chopped spring onion	1 Tbsp
Egg	1, beaten
Cooking oil for frying	

GREEN CHILLI SAUCE

Green chillies	100 g (3¹/₂ oz), seeded
Water	1 Tbsp
Salt	¹/₂ tsp

GARNISH

Fried shallots (page 11)	3 Tbsp
Chopped coriander leaves	1 cup
Chopped Chinese celery	1 cup

1. Make spice paste first. Grind ginger and garlic together with 3 Tbsp water in a food processor. Add ground spices and mix well.

2. To make soup, heat oil in a saucepan and sauté onion and whole spices until onion is a golden brown. Add spice paste and fry until oil surfaces. Add lemon grass, chicken, stock and salt and bring the pot to the boil. Turn down heat and simmer for 30 minutes until chicken is cooked. The time depends on the size of chicken pieces.

3. Remove chicken from soup and when cool enough to handle, shred chicken and set aside with other garnishes. Return bones to the soup and simmer for another 10 minutes.

4. Prepare *bergedel*. Mix mashed potato, salt and spring onion and form into 6 patties. Dip patties into the beaten egg and fry in hot oil until nicely brown.

5. Fry remainder of beaten egg in the oil, then slice finely for garnish.

6. Prepare green chilli sauce. Put all sauce ingredients together into a food processor and blend until fine. Bottle green chilli sauce.

7. To serve noodles, bring a pot of water to the boil and blanch bean sprouts for 10 seconds. Scoop out and drain well. Divide and place into serving bowls.

8. Return water to the boil and blanch noodles until tender but al dente. Scoop out and drain well. Divide and place into serving bowls.

9. Ladle hot soup over noodles and garnish with shredded chicken, *bergedel*, sliced egg, fried shallots and chopped herbs. Serve green chilli sauce on the side for those who like it hot.

Fried Glass Noodles with Crabmeat

Preparation time: 30 minutes   Serves 5–6

The preparation time will be at least 2 hours if you use freshly shelled crabmeat. Simplify this dish by using ready-shelled crabmeat or peeled prawns. If only enjoying crabmeat did not take so much work! Of course, if you are preparing a special treat...

Shallot oil (page 11)	3 Tbsp
Water	125 ml (4 fl oz / $^1/_2$ cup)
Chopped garlic	1 Tbsp
Light soy sauce	4 Tbsp
Dark soy sauce	1 tsp
Salt	$^1/_2$ tsp
Glass noodles	500 g (1 lb 1$^1/_2$ oz), softened in cold water
Crabmeat	400 g (14$^1/_3$ oz)
Ground black pepper	2 tsp
Fried shallots (page 11)	2 Tbsp
Coriander leaves	1 large bunch, chopped
Spring onions	3, chopped

1. Heat shallot oil in a wok and fry garlic until fragrant. Add water, soy sauces and salt. Stir well and add glass noodles. Mix well.
2. Fry for about 3 minutes. If noodles dry out too quickly, add a bit more water.
3. Mix in crabmeat, pepper and fried shallots and lastly chopped coriander leaves and spring onions.
4. Dish out and serve hot.

Thai Seafood Rice Soup

Preparation time: 2 hours   Serves 5–6

This seafood rice soup wins points for richness of flavour and effort. Pick seafood that suits your budget and personal taste, but make sure there are some trimmings for boiling the stock. If using live shellfish such as clams, boil it lightly first and extract the meat. Discard the last 2-cm (³/₄-in) of the boiling liquid because of the grit and use the rest for stock. Cooked rice for rice soup should be soft but not watery.

Assorted seafood	1 kg (2 lb 3 oz)
Chicken stock (page 20)	1 litre (32 fl oz / 4 cups)
Garlic oil (page 11)	to taste
Fried garlic (page 11)	to taste
Fish sauce	to taste
Cooked long-grain rice	4 cups (from 300 g / 11 oz / 2 rice cooker cups rice)

SEAFOOD STOCK

Water	1 litre (32 fl oz / 4 cups)
Garlic	1 head, rinsed and smashed
Chinese celery	1 large bunch, coarsely chopped
Coriander leaves (cilantro)	1 large bunch, coarsely chopped
Salt	1 tsp
Red bird's eye chillies	3, halved
White vinegar	1 Tbsp
Fish sauce	2 Tbsp

GARNISH AND CONDIMENTS

Coriander leaves, spring onion, Chinese celery, basil leaves, fried garlic and garlic oil (page 11)

Lime wedges

Red chillies with fish sauce (page 15) or vinegar-chilli dip (page 16)

1. Start by cleaning seafood. If using squid, remove ink sacs. Prawns may be peeled and deveined, leaving the tails on. Remove top half of crabs and discard gills. Halve or quarter crabs depending on size of crabs and number of guests. Bone fish. Keep seafood trimmings for stock.

2. Combine seafood trimmings with other ingredients for seafood stock in a large pot. Bring to the boil, then lower heat and simmer for 30 minutes. Strain stock and discard solids.

3. Combine chicken and seafood stock. Add garlic oil, fried garlic and fish sauce to taste and bring to the boil. Add trimmed seafood to boiling stock and simmer until seafood changes colour.

4. To serve, spoon some rice into a deep dish bowl and ladle seafood stock over. Garnish and serve immediately with saucers of red chillies with fish sauce.

Arroz Caldo (Filipino Rice Soup)

Preparation time: 1½ hours   Serves 5–6

This is a Filipino chicken soup served with soft rice. The Spanish term means "rice soup". Prepare extra vegetables to add to the soup after the chicken soup has been made. This rice soup can also be spiced with red chillies, if preferred, and calamansi limes substituted with white vinegar.

Celery	2 stalks, stringed and sliced 1-cm (½-in) thick
Fresh peas	110 g (4 oz / 1 cup)
Tomatoes	100 g (3½ oz), cut into small wedges
White short-grain rice	200 g (7 oz / 1 cup / 1⅓ rice cooker cups)
White glutinous rice	50 g (1⅔ oz / ¼ cup / ⅓ rice cooker cup)
Water	625 ml (20 fl oz / 2½ cups)

CHICKEN SOUP

Chicken	750 g (1 lb 11 oz)
Chicken bones	500 g (1 lb 1½ oz)
Onion	50 g (1⅔ oz), peeled and quartered
Tomatoes	100 g (3½ oz), quartered
Garlic	4 cloves, peeled and smashed
Fish sauce	2 Tbsp
Cracked black peppercorns	½ Tbsp
Water	2.5 litres (80 fl oz / 10 cups)
Coriander leaves	1 small bunch
Spring onion	1, small
Chinese celery	1 small bunch

GARNISH

Chopped spring onion
Chopped coriander leaves
Fish sauce
Ground black pepper/chopped red chillies
Calamansi lime halves/vinegar

1. Put all chicken soup ingredients into a stockpot and bring to the boil. Skim off any scum that rises to the top. Turn down heat and simmer for 45 minutes.

2. Remove chicken, leave to cool, then shred meat. Set meat aside in a covered bowl to prevent it from crusting up, or immerse meat in some stock. Return bones to stockpot and simmer for another 30 minutes. Strain stock and discard solids.

3. Bring soup to the boil and add celery and peas. Simmer for 5 minutes before adding tomatoes. Remove from heat once soup comes to the boil.

4. Combine short-grain and glutinous rice with 625 ml (20 fl oz / 2½ cups) water and cook using your preferred method.

5. To serve rice soup, dish rice out into deep dishes and ladle hot soup and vegetables over. Garnish with shredded chicken, spring onion, coriander leaves, and a drizzle of fish sauce. Have pepper/chillies and lime halves/vinegar on the side.

Ada Polo (Persian Rice and Lentils)

Preparation time: 2 hours   Serves 5–6

Pre-cook the lentils or chickpeas overnight in a slow-cooker in lieu of soaking. Double the amount and freeze what is not needed for another day. You can also use a quick-cooking dhal like mung or masoor if you don't mind a more mushy result. Note that dried beans that have been stored for a long time take more time to soften.

Lentils/dhal	300 g (11 oz / 1½ cups)
Ghee/cooking oil	3 Tbsp
Onions	100 g (3½ oz), peeled and chopped
Minced meat (lamb/beef/chicken)	200 g (7 oz)
Advieh/Indian garam masala (page 12)	1 tsp
Salt	2 tsp
Water	1.25 litres (40 fl oz / 5 cups)
Basmati rice	450 g (1 lb / 2¼ cups / 3 rice cooker cups), soaked 1 hour
West Asian dates	100 g (3½ oz / ½ cup), pitted and sliced
Raisins	100 g (3½ oz / ½ cup)

GARNISH AND CONDIMENTS

Lemon wedges

Chopped coriander leaves/ parsley

Pickled vegetables (page 25)

Cooked yoghurt sauce (page 19)

1. Boil lentils/dhal until just soft. Drain and set aside.
2. Heat ghee/oil in a frying pan and fry onions until they begin to brown. Add minced meat, advieh/garam masala and ½ tsp salt. Continue frying for about 2 minutes. Add 250 ml (8 fl oz / 1 cup) water and bring to the boil. Turn down heat and simmer until meat is tender and there is still about 4 Tbsp gravy left.
3. Combine rice with cooked lentils/dhal, dates, raisins, remaining salt and remaining water and cook rice using your preferred method. When rice is done, stir meat and gravy into rice. Cover and rest rice for 10 minutes before serving.
4. Garnish pilaf with lemon wedges and chopped coriander/parsley. Serve with pickled vegetables and cooked yoghurt sauce.

Nasi Ulam (Malay Rice Salad)

Preparation time: 1 hour   Serves 5–6

This Malay, Indonesian or Straits Chinese one-dish meal is a good budget meal as the rice can be dressed with just salted fish and vegetables, and also with fresh fish if the budget allows or the occasion calls for it.

Dried salted fish (threadfin)	100 g (3¹/₂ oz)
Cooking oil for frying	
Fish	100 g (3¹/₂ oz)
Salt	¹/₂ tsp
Cabbage	300 g (11 oz), finely shredded
Warm cooked long-grain rice	4 cups (from 300 g / 11 oz / 2 rice cooker cups rice)
Cucumber	400 g (14¹/₃ oz), cored and cubed
Assorted herbs (turmeric leaves, *kencur* leaves, young galangal leaves, mint, kaffir lime leaves, shredded torch ginger bud, coriander leaves, spring onions,)	2 cups, chopped or finely shredded

DRESSING

Sambal belacan (page 13)	1¹/₂ Tbsp
Shallots	100 g (3¹/₂ oz), peeled and thinly sliced
Lime juice	3 Tbsp
Salt	1 tsp
Toasted grated coconut (page 10)	1 Tbsp

1. Rinse salted fish and wipe dry. Slice thinly. Heat some oil in a frying pan and fry salted fish over low heat until crisp. Pull out any bones and pound until fine. Set aside.

2. Rub fish with ¹/₂ tsp salt and fry in hot oil until cooked. Cool and flake fish, discarding any bones.

3. To make dressing, combine ingredients with shredded cabbage. Adjust seasoning to taste before mixing into rice.

4. Stir dressing into warm rice with pounded salted fish, fish flakes, cucumber and chopped herbs.

5. Serve warm or cold.

Nasi Urap (Indonesian Rice and Coconut Salad)

Preparation time: 1½ hours   Serves 5–6

The vegetable selection can be kept raw or lightly blanched or a combination of raw and blanched. Any fried fish can be used, including dried anchovies (*ikan bilis*) which some cooks fry up and bottle as a quick snack or side dish to go with rice porridge or rice. The common yellow-banded scad (*ikan kuning*) is tasty and cheap to boot.

Yellow-banded scad (*ikan kuning*)	750 g (1 lb 11 oz), or 500 g (1 lb 1½ oz) dried anchovies, heads and innards removed
Salt (for scad)	½ tsp
Ground turmeric (for scad)	1 tsp
Cooking oil for frying	
Bean sprouts	300 g (11 oz), tails removed and blanched
Water convolvulus	500 g (1 lb 1½ oz), blanched and tied into bundles
Long beans	300 g (11 oz), cut into finger lengths and blanched
Assorted herbs (spring onions, coriander leaves, turmeric leaves, *kencur* leaves, young galangal leaves, mint, kaffir lime leaves, shredded torch ginger bud)	2 cups, chopped/finely shredded
Fresh white grated coconut or toasted grated coconut (page 10)	250 g (9 oz)
Warm cooked long-grain rice	4 cups (from 300 g / 11 oz / 2 rice cooker cups rice)

DRESSING

Galangal/kencur	5 slices
Garlic	5 cloves, peeled
Sambal belacan (page 13)	2 Tbsp
Kaffir lime/*kencur*/turmeric leaves	4–6, finely shredded
Shallots	100 g (3½ oz), thinly sliced
Salt	1½ tsp

1. Start by preparing fish. If using yellow-banded scad (*ikan kuning*), gut it, then rub inside of stomach with some salt to clean it well. If scad is large, make a couple of slits on the bulkiest part of fish so that it will fry well. Mix salt and ground turmeric and rub on cleaned fish. Stand for 15 minutes. Heat some oil in a wok and fry fish, a few at a time, until nicely brown on both sides.

2. If using dried anchovies, rinse under a running tap. Drain, then pat very dry with a paper towel. Heat some oil in a wok and fry dried anchovies over low heat, stirring constantly, until crisp.

3. Bring a pot of water to the boil and blanch bean sprouts for 10 seconds, water convolvulus for 5 seconds and long beans for 10–15 seconds.

4. Make dressing. Pound galangal/*kencur* with garlic and *sambal belacan*. When fine, mix into blanched bean sprouts, assorted herbs, shallots and salt. The fresh grated or toasted coconut can also be mixed with some of the dressing or kept separate.

5. Arrange dressed bean sprouts, fried fish, vegetables, grated coconut and cooked rice on a large serving platter for guests to help themselves.

Black Dhal Biryani

Preparation time: 2 hours   Serves 5–6

This biryani or pilaf can be made with a meat-flavoured stock, vegetable stock or water. To make a vegetable stock, substitute meat bones with flavourful vegetables such as celery, tomatoes and carrots. It can also be made cheaper by substituting saffron with ground turmeric sprinkled directly into the hot rice. Another cheap substitute for saffron is safflower.

Chicken/lamb/beef bones	750 g (1 lb 11 oz)
Cinnamon stick	6-cm (2.5-in) length
Cardamoms	4 pods
Cloves	4
Ginger	5-cm (2-in) knob, peeled
Water	1.25 ml (40 fl oz / 5 cups)
Basmati rice	450 g (1 lb / 2^1/$_4$ cups / 3 rice cooker cups), soaked 1 hour
Salt	1 tsp
Indian garam masala/baharat (page 12)	^{1}/$_2$ tsp
Saffron (optional)	^{1}/$_2$ tsp, soaked in 1 Tbsp water
Tomatoes	50 g (1^2/$_3$ oz), skinned and thinly sliced
Green chillies	3, seeded and chopped
Mint	^{1}/$_2$ cup, chopped
Coriander leaves	^{1}/$_2$ cup, chopped

DHAL CURRY

Ghee	3 Tbsp
Onion	50 g (1^2/$_3$ oz), peeled and thinly sliced
Black dhal	250 g (9 oz / 1^1/$_4$ cups), soaked overnight
Water	750 ml (24 fl oz / 3 cups)
Salt	^{1}/$_2$ tsp
Potatoes	150 g (5^1/$_3$ oz), peeled and cubed
Tomatoes	100 g (3^1/$_2$ oz), chopped
Green chillies	3, seeded and chopped
Yoghurt	4 Tbsp

SPICE PASTE FOR DHAL CURRY

Ginger	5-cm (2-in) knob, peeled and thinly sliced
Garlic	2 cloves, peeled and thinly sliced
Ground turmeric	^{1}/$_2$ tsp
Chilli powder	1 tsp

CONDIMENTS

Pickled vegetables (page 25)
Cucumber raita (page 18)
Yoghurt dip (page 19)

1. Make spiced stock for cooking rice the day before or several days ahead so it will be cold enough to measure out. It also freezes well. Combine meat bones with cinnamon, cardamoms, cloves and ginger with water and bring to the boil. If making a spiced vegetable stock, combine spices with about 1 kg (2 lb 3 oz) of your chosen vegetables and bring to the boil. Turn down heat and simmer for an hour. Cool, discard solids and measure out 940 ml (30 fl oz / 3³/₄ cups) stock for cooking rice. Keep remaining stock for sauce or another biryani.

2. Prepare dhal curry next. Make spice paste by pounding together ginger and garlic to a fine paste. Mix paste with ground turmeric and chilli powder.

3. Melt ghee in a saucepan and fry onion until golden brown. Scoop out and set aside. To the same pan, add spice paste and fry until fragrant. Add dhal, 750 ml (24 fl oz / 3 cups) water and ¹/₂ tsp salt and bring to the boil. Turn down heat and simmer for 30 minutes before adding potatoes. Continue simmering until dhal is tender.

4. Add tomatoes and chillies and simmer for another 10 minutes. The dhal curry should be very thick, not watery. If there is too much liquid, boil some of it off or scoop out for use in cooking rice. Stir in yoghurt and bring to the boil. Remove from heat.

5. Combine rice, spiced stock and salt and cook rice using your preferred method. When rice is cooked, fluff it up and stir in garam masala/baharat and fried onion, followed by soaked saffron with its soaking liquid if using.

6. Combine cooked rice, dhal and two-thirds of chopped green chillies, mint and coriander leaves in a large casserole and bake in a 120°C (250°F) oven for 10 minutes or combine in the rice cooker if large enough. Just before serving, garnish with the remainder of the chopped chillies and herbs.

7. Serve rice hot with pickled vegetables and a cucumber raita or yoghurt dip with vegetable sticks.

Persian Cherry Rice

Preparation time: 2 hours   Serves 5–6

In ancient Persian, cherries were once called "fruit of the king". So this dish is definitely a festive one. As fresh cherries are usually exported as fruit, they tend to be more sweet than sour or only mildly tart. If using fresh fruit cherries, omit the sugar. If using dried sour cherries, make sure they have not been sweetened artificially. Look for unsweetened dried fruit in the organic foods section of supermarkets or stores specialising in organic foods. Or substitute fresh sour cherries with fresh or frozen cranberries.

Chicken thighs or drumsticks	6 pieces or about 750 g (1 lb 11 oz), skinned
Dried sour cherries	200 g (7 oz)
Water	2 litres (64 fl oz / 8 cups)
Ghee	3 Tbsp
Onion	50 g (1²/₃ oz), peeled and finely chopped
Garlic	1 clove, peeled and chopped
Tomato	50 g (1²/₃ oz), chopped
Advieh (page 12)	2 tsp
Lemon juice	to taste
Sugar	to taste
Salt	1¹/₂ tsp
Basmati rice	450 g (1 lb / 2¹/₄ cups / 3 rice cooker cups), soaked 1 hour
Cornflour (optional)	1–2 Tbsp

MARINADE FOR CHICKEN

Ground turmeric	¹/₂ tsp
Salt	1 tsp
Ground black pepper	¹/₂ tsp

GARNISH

Lemon wedges
Chopped parsley/mint

1. Combine marinade ingredients and rub on chicken. Stand for 1 hour.

2. Cherries need to be stoned and boiled whether they are fresh or dried. Rinse cherries clean and boil in 2 litres (64 fl oz / 8 cups) water until soft. Cool, then stone cherries. Cherries can be kept whole or chopped coarsely. Keep cherry water for cooking chicken but get rid of any grit. Let water settle, then slowly pour out all but the last 0.5 cm (¹/₄ in) of the water.

3. To prepare chicken, melt ghee in a saucepan and brown onion. Add garlic and tomato and fry until fragrant. Stir in advieh, then add chicken and cherry water and bring to the boil. Lower heat and simmer until chicken is cooked. Add lemon juice and sugar to taste and ¹/₂ tsp salt. The chicken should taste more sour than sweet. There should be a rich-coloured gravy.

4. Leaving at least 250 ml (8 fl oz / 1 cup) of gravy with chicken, measure out 940 ml (30 fl oz / 3³/₄ cups) for cooking rice. Top up with water if insufficient.

5. Combine gravy, rice, half the stoned cherries and remaining 1 tsp salt and cook rice using your preferred method. When rice is done, fluff it up and scoop half into a large casserole. Spread chicken pieces and half of remaining cherries over rice, then cover chicken and cherries with rest of rice. Bake covered casserole in a 120°C (250°F) oven for 10 minutes.

6. Make a sauce with remainder of gravy and cherries. Using a stick blender, blend fruit with gravy. Adjust seasoning to taste. The gravy can be further thickened with some cornflour mixed with a bit of water and brought to the boil.

7. Serve cherry rice garnished with lemon wedges, a sprinkling of chopped parsley/mint and cherry sauce.

Sabzi Polo (Persian Herb Rice)

Preparation time: 45 minutes   Serves 5–6

This traditional Iranian New Year dish is a refreshing mix of green and white and perfect for people who enjoy the flavour of fresh herbs. Stir the herbs into the rice only when the rice is cooked and just before serving the rice. More herbs can be served as a salad. Double or treble the amount of herbs and serve the mixed herbs as a salad, another traditional Persian side dish.

Basmati rice	450 g (1 lb / 2¼ cups / 3 rice cooker cups), soaked 1 hour
Salt	1½ tsp
Leeks	300 g (11 oz), thinly sliced
Water	940 ml (30 fl oz / 3¾ cups)
Ghee	4 Tbsp
Fresh herbs (dill, mint, coriander leaves, chives, spring onions, thyme, parsley, fenugreek leaves)	4 cups, chopped
Cooked yoghurt sauce (page 19)	

1. Cook rice with salt, leeks and water using your preferred method.

2. When rice is done, fluff it up and stir ghee and chopped herbs into rice.

3. If a rice crust or *tah deeg* is desired, stir in the herbs only after the *tah deeg* has been made. To get a rice crust, melt the ghee and stir into the rice. Bake the rice in the rice pot or over very low heat for 10 minutes to form the crust. Then stir in the herbs.

4. Serve herb rice with cooked yoghurt sauce and grilled lamb or chicken (page 23).

Shirini Polo (Persian Chicken Pilaf)

Preparation time: 1 hour   Serves 5–6

This is pilaf on the fly. Make it to use up any leftover grilled or roasted chicken or turkey or get a ready-grilled chicken. Perk the rice with whatever dried fruit and nuts you may have in the larder. Jazz up the flavour with orange flower water or rose water. Or use artificial rose essence which is found in many Asian larders. If used very sparingly, it can be quite good.

Ghee	3 Tbsp
Cinnamon stick	4-cm (1$^{1}/_{2}$-in) length
Sultanas	30 g (1 oz / $^{1}/_{4}$ cup)
Slivered pistachios	30 g (1 oz / $^{1}/_{4}$ cup)
Slivered almonds	30 g (1 oz / $^{1}/_{4}$ cup)
Cooked chicken/turkey	500 g (1 lb 1$^{1}/_{2}$ oz / 2$^{1}/_{2}$ cups)
Lemon juice	2 Tbsp
Sugar	2 tsp
Basmati rice	450 g (1 lb / 2$^{1}/_{4}$ cups / 3 rice cooker cups), soaked 1 hour
Advieh (page 12)	$^{1}/_{2}$ tsp
Water	940 ml (30 fl oz / 3$^{3}/_{4}$ cups)
Salt	1$^{1}/_{2}$ tsp
Orange flower water/rose water (optional)	$^{1}/_{2}$ Tbsp
Chopped mint/parsley	

CONDIMENTS
Pickled vegetables (page 25)
Cooked yoghurt sauce (page 19)

1. Melt ghee in a frying pan and fry cinnamon stick, sultanas, nuts and cooked chicken/turkey. Add lemon juice and sugar and fry until sugar has dissolved. Adjust seasoning to taste. Remove cinnamon stick for cooking with rice.

2. Combine rice with cinnamon stick, advieh, water and salt and cook rice using your preferred method. When rice is done, fluff it up and stir in orange flower water/rose water if using.

3. Either layer rice and chicken mixture or stir chicken mixture into rice in a casserole. Bake for 10 minutes in a 120°C (250°F) oven. Leave to stand for 10 minutes before serving.

4. Garnish with mint/parsley. Serve with pickled vegetables or cooked yoghurt sauce.

Indian Vegetarian Pilaf

Preparation time: 45 minutes   Serves 5–6

The vegetables used in this pilaf can be any of your choice, but it should include a generous serving of peas, beans or boiled dhal to put some protein into the meal. Decrease the water for the rice if you are using juicy vegetables.

Ghee	85 ml (2^1/$_2$ fl oz / ^{1}/$_3$ cup)
Onions	100 g (3^1/$_2$ oz), chopped
Tomatoes	200 g (7 oz), thickly sliced
Potatoes	100 g (3^1/$_2$ oz), peeled and cubed
Mixed vegetables	750 g (1 lb 9^1/$_2$ oz), cut into small pieces
Long-grain brown rice	450 g (1 lb / 2^1/$_4$ cups / 3 rice cooker cups)
Salt	1^1/$_2$ tsp
Sugar	^{1}/$_2$ tsp
Water	1 litre (32 fl oz / 4 cups)

SPICE PASTE

Ginger	5-cm (2-in) knob, peeled and thinly sliced
Ground turmeric	^{1}/$_2$ tsp
Chilli powder	1 tsp

WHOLE SPICES

Cumin seeds	1 tsp
Cloves	4
Indian bay leaves	2
Green cardamom	4 pods
Cinnamon stick	4-cm (1^1/$_2$-in) length

CONDIMENTS

Pickled vegetables (page 25)

Cooked yoghurt sauce
  (page 19)

1. Prepare spice paste. Pound or blend ginger with 2 Tbsp water until fine. Mix with ground turmeric and chilli powder to get a thick paste.

2. Heat ghee and fry onions with cumin seeds until onions are transparent. Add rest of whole spices and spice paste and fry until fragrant. Stir in tomatoes, potatoes and vegetables and fry for 2 minutes. Add a little water if vegetables are dry ones like carrots or peas.

3. Combine rice, salt, sugar and water and mix well before adding vegetables. Cook rice using your preferred method. When rice is done, fluff it up and mix well. Rest rice for 10 minutes.

4. Serve pilaf with pickled vegetables or cooked yoghurt sauce.

Timman Z'affaran (Iraqi Saffron Rice)

Preparation time: 1½ hours   Serves 5–6

This rice smells heavenly when it is being cooked because of the rose water. However, this smell evaporates and you have to sprinkle more rose water into the rice just before serving. If using minced mutton or lamb, first simmer the meat until tender. Alternatively tenderise with a large pinch of bicarbonate of soda. Saffron can be substituted with ground turmeric or safflower to reduce the cost of making this dish.

Rose water	2 Tbsp
Saffron	1 tsp
Ghee	4 Tbsp
Almonds	10, halved
Onions	100 g (3½ oz), peeled and thinly sliced
Minced lamb/mutton/ chicken cubes	250 g (9 oz)
Salt	1½ tsp
Baharat (page 12)	2 tsp
Golden raisins	30 g (1 oz / ¼ cup)
Fresh peas	100 g (3½ oz)
Basmati rice	450 g (1 lb / 2¼ cups / 3 rice cooker cups)
Water	1.2 litres (38 fl oz / 4¾ cups)
Chopped parsley	1 cup

CONDIMENTS

Cooked yoghurt sauce (page 19)
Garlic/onion yoghurt dip
   (page 19)

1. Mix rose water with saffron threads and set aside.
2. Heat 2 Tbsp ghee in a wok and brown split almonds. Remove and set aside for garnishing.
3. Stir in sliced onions and fry until soft and transparent, then stir in minced meat, ½ tsp salt and baharat. Fry until meat changes colour. Add 250 ml (8 fl oz / 1 cup) water and simmer until meat is tender and just moist. Add raisins and peas and cook for another 2 minutes.
4. Combine rice with 940 ml (30 fl oz / 3¾ cups) water, remaining salt and half the rose water-saffron mixture and cook rice using your preferred method. When rice is done, fluff it up and stir meat and chopped parsley into rice. Cover and rest rice for 10 minutes before serving.
5. To serve rice, dish out into a large serving plate. Sprinkle remaining rose water saffron mixture on rice and garnish with browned almonds.
6. Serve with a cooked yoghurt sauce or yoghurt dip with vegetable sticks.

Green Coriander Rice with Eggs

Preparation time: 45 minutes   Serves 5–6

This is an economical yet festive dish. Instead of meat, this flavoured rice is served with boiled eggs. Costs can be further reduced by substituting ghee with oil and the more expensive Basmati rice with any cheaper long-grain rice. Use waxy potatoes as they hold their shape better.

Ghee	3 Tbsp
Potatoes	200 g (7 oz), peeled and cubed
Onion	50 g (1²/₃ oz), peeled and thinly sliced
Tomato	50 g (1²/₃ oz), thickly sliced
Yoghurt	125 ml (4 fl oz / ¹/₂ cup)
Basmati rice	450 g (1 lb / 2¹/₄ cups / 3 rice cooker cups), soaked 1 hour
Water	940 ml (30 fl oz / 3³/₄ cups)
Salt	1¹/₂ tsp
Indian garam masala (page 12)	¹/₂ tsp
Hard-boiled eggs	10, peeled and halved

SPICE PASTE

Coriander leaves	1 cup
Onion	25 g (1 oz), peeled and chopped
Green chillies	50 g (1²/₃ oz), seeded
Ginger	5-cm (2-in) knob, peeled and sliced
Garlic	3 cloves, peeled
Water	2 Tbsp

WHOLE SPICES

Cinnamon stick	4-cm (1¹/₂-in) length
Green cardamom	4 pods
Indian bay leaves	2

GARNISH AND CONDIMENTS

Coriander leaves	¹/₂ cup, chopped
Cucumber raita (page 18)	
Pickled vegetables (page 25)	

1. Make spice paste. Blend spice paste ingredients together into a fine paste.
2. Heat ghee in a frying pan and brown potato cubes. The potato does not need to be cooked through. Set aside.
3. In the same pan, fry onion until golden brown. Set aside. Reheat pan and fry whole spices for 1 minute. Add spice paste and fry until oil surfaces. Stir in tomato and fry until oil surfaces again. Add yoghurt, mix well and cook for 2 minutes.
4. Combine yoghurt mixture with rice, water, potatoes and salt and cook rice using your preferred method. When rice is done, fluff it up and stir in fried onion and garam masala. Rest rice for 10 minutes.
5. To serve, stir coriander leaves into hot rice. Dish out and top with hard-boiled egg. Serve with a cucumber raita or pickled vegetables.

Maqloobeh (West Asian Upside-down Rice)

Preparation time: 45 minutes   Serves 5–6

This home-cooked dish is actually good enough for company and easy to put together. If available, use a hard rice like Uncle Ben's parboiled rice or brown rice so that the rice stays firm.

Chicken with bone	750 g (1 lb 11 oz), cut into 6 pieces
Salt	2 tsp
Baharat (page 12)	1 tsp
Olive oil	4 Tbsp
Aubergines	100 g (3½ oz), cut into 1-cm (½-in) thick slices
Onions	100 g (3½ oz), peeled and finely chopped
Red and green capsicums (bell peppers)	1 each, seeded and cut into thick strips
Long-grain brown rice	450 g (1 lb / 2¼ cups / 3 rice cooker cups)
Water	1 litre (32 fl oz / 4 cups)

GARNISH
Chopped parsley
Toasted almond halves/pine nuts

1. Rub chicken with 1 tsp salt and baharat.
2. Heat a heavy frying pan. Brush a little olive oil on it and brown aubergine slices. Set aside.
3. Heat remainder of olive oil in a large saucepan and brown chicken. Stir in chopped onions and fry until onions are brown.
4. Layer the bottom of the rice pot/pan with the chicken mixture, aubergines and capsicums. Top with rice, remaining salt and water. Cook rice using your preferred method. To prevent the vegetables from floating up, put a small plate or a round wire rack over the rice.
5. Rest rice for 10 minutes before turning it over. To turn it over, cover the rice pot/pan with a serving plate. With oven gloves on or protecting your hands with a thick dishcloth in each hand, turn the rice pot/pan over, pressing pot/pan and plate tightly together as you turn.
6. Garnish with chopped parsley and toasted almond halves/pine nuts.

Tabyeet (Jewish Slow-cooked Chicken with Rice)

Preparation time: 45 minutes   Serves 5–6

Tabyeet means "cooked overnight" in Arabic and this Jewish Sabbath dish from Iraq is cooked when the sun goes down on Friday and eaten when the sun sets the next evening on the Sabbath. If available, use a hard rice such as Uncle Ben's parboiled rice. The slow baking turns regular long-grain a little mushy especially near the bottom. Tabyeet is traditionally baked in a slow oven.

Olive oil	3 Tbsp
Chicken thighs or drumsticks	5 pieces, about 750 g (1 lb 11 oz)
Onions	50 g (1²/₃ oz), peeled and thickly sliced
Tomatoes	200 g (7 oz), cut into thick wedges
Basmati rice	450 g (1 lb / 2¹/₄ cups / 3 rice cooker cups)
Green cardamom	6 pods
Eggs	3
Water	875 ml (28 fl oz / 3¹/₂ cups)
Pickled vegetables (page 25)	

SPICE MIX

Baharat (page 12)	3 tsp
Parsley	1 cup, chopped
Salt	2 tsp
Ground cumin	¹/₂ tsp

1. Prepare spice mix. Mix together baharat, parsley, salt and ground cumin. Divide into 3 equal parts. Rub one part into chicken, mix another part with onions and tomatoes, and the last part with rice.

2. Line the bottom of a slow cooker with olive oil and cardamoms. Top with chicken, then layer with half the onions and tomatoes. Rinse eggs clean and tuck them in with onions and tomatoes. Add rice and top with remaining onions and tomatoes.

3. Pour water gently into slow cooker. Cover and leave to cook overnight (8 hours).

4. The dish can also be baked in a 120°C (250°F) oven overnight (8 hours). The baking dish should have a lid and the lid can be sealed with dough made of flour and water.

5. If the rice is baked, it will have a rice crust. To loosen the rice crust, soak the bottom of the pot in cold water or place on a very damp towel for 10 minutes.

6. Loosen rice with a flat spatula before turning dish over onto a serving platter. Serve with pickled vegetables.

Sayadieh (Syrian-Lebanese Rice and Fish)

Preparation time: 2 hours   Serves 5–6

Found in the Mediterranean coastal regions of Lebanon and Syria where fish, while expensive, is eaten more frequently than in the regions away from the coast, *sayadieh* makes a good festive dish. This recipe gives a strong-tasting rice because it uses fish stock. If a lighter flavour is preferred, dilute the fish stock with water or use less fish scraps to make the stock.

Boneless fish fillets	750 g (1 lb 11 oz), cut into large cubes
Baharat	2 tsp
Lemon juice	1 Tbsp
Salt	2 tsp
Olive oil	125 ml (4 fl oz / $^1/_2$ cup)
Pine nuts	50 g (1$^2/_3$ oz / $^1/_2$ cup)
Onions	200 g (7 oz), peeled and thinly sliced
Long-grain rice	450 g (1 lb / 2$^1/_4$ cups / 3 rice cooker cups)
Parsley	$^1/_4$ cup, chopped
Fish stock	940 ml (30 fl oz / 3$^3/_4$ cups)
Lemon wedges	
Pickled vegetables (page 25)	

FISH STOCK

Fish trimmings	500 g (1 lb 1$^1/_2$ oz)
Parsley	1 bunch
Garlic	1 clove, peeled and smashed
Water	1.5 litres (48 fl oz / 6 cups)

SAUCE

Lemon juice	1 Tbsp
Salt	$^1/_2$ tsp
Cornflour (optional)	1–1$^1/_2$ Tbsp
Flat-leaf parsley	$^1/_4$ cup, chopped

1. Rub fish with baharat, lemon juice and $^1/_2$ salt. Set aside for 30 minutes.
2. Heat olive oil in a frying pan and brown pine nuts. Scoop out and set aside. Stir in onions and cook to a golden-dark brown colour, but do not let it burn. Scoop out and reserve one-quarter for garnishing.
3. To make fish stock, combine fried onions with fish stock ingredients in a pot and boil for 30 minutes until stock turns brown and onions are mushy and pale. Strain away solids. Measure out 940 ml (30 fl oz / 3$^3/_4$ cups) stock for cooking rice. Keep remainder for making sauce.
4. Combine fish stock with rice and 1$^1/_2$ tsp salt and cook rice using your preferred method.
5. In the same oil in which onions were fried, fry fish on both sides until done.

6. Strain oil to get rid of any solids and use it to make sauce. If it is less than 1 Tbsp, top up. To make sauce, combine oil, fish stock for sauce, lemon juice and salt and bring to the boil. If desired, thicken sauce with cornflour mixed with a little water. Add cornflour mixture to fish stock and bring to the boil, stirring in parsley when it thickens.

7. To serve, top individual plates of rice with pieces of fish and a garnish of fried onion and pine nuts. The sauce may be poured directly on the rice or kept on the side in a sauce boat. Serve with lemon wedges and pickles.

Weights and Measures

Quantities for this book are given in Metric, Imperial and American (spoon) measures.
Standard spoon and cup measurements used are: 1 tsp = 5 ml, 1 Tbsp = 15 ml, 1 cup = 250 ml.
All measures are level unless otherwise stated.

Liquid and Volume Measures

Metric	Imperial	American
5 ml	$^1/_6$ fl oz	1 teaspoon
10 ml	$^1/_3$ fl oz	1 dessertspoon
15 ml	$^1/_2$ fl oz	1 tablespoon
60 ml	2 fl oz	$^1/_4$ cup (4 tablespoons)
85 ml	$2^1/_2$ fl oz	$^1/_3$ cup
90 ml	3 fl oz	$^3/_8$ cup (6 tablespoons)
125 ml	4 fl oz	$^1/_2$ cup
180 ml	6 fl oz	$^3/_4$ cup
250 ml	8 fl oz	1 cup
300 ml	10 fl oz ($^1/_2$ pint)	$1^1/_4$ cups
375 ml	12 fl oz	$1^1/_2$ cups
435 ml	14 fl oz	$1^3/_4$ cups
500 ml	16 fl oz	2 cups
625 ml	20 fl oz (1 pint)	$2^1/_2$ cups
750 ml	24 fl oz ($1^1/_5$ pints)	3 cups
1 litre	32 fl oz ($1^3/_5$ pints)	4 cups
1.25 litres	40 fl oz (2 pints)	5 cups
1.5 litres	48 fl oz ($2^2/_5$ pints)	6 cups
2.5 litres	80 fl oz (4 pints)	10 cups

Dry Measures

Metric	Imperial
30 grams	1 ounce
45 grams	$1^1/_2$ ounces
55 grams	2 ounces
70 grams	$2^1/_2$ ounces
85 grams	3 ounces
100 grams	$3^1/_2$ ounces
110 grams	4 ounces
125 grams	$4^1/_2$ ounces
140 grams	5 ounces
280 grams	10 ounces
450 grams	16 ounces (1 pound)
500 grams	1 pound, $1^1/_2$ ounces
700 grams	$1^1/_2$ pounds
800 grams	$1^3/_4$ pounds
1 kilogram	2 pounds, 3 ounces
1.5 kilograms	3 pounds, $4^1/_2$ ounces
2 kilograms	4 pounds, 6 ounces

Oven Temperature

	°C	°F	Gas Regulo
Very slow	120	250	1
Slow	150	300	2
Moderately slow	160	325	3
Moderate	180	350	4
Moderately hot	190/200	370/400	5/6
Hot	210/220	410/440	6/7
Very hot	230	450	8

Length

Metric	Imperial
0.5 cm	$^1/_4$ inch
1 cm	$^1/_2$ inch
1.5 cm	$^3/_4$ inch
2.5 cm	1 inch